wavelength

Tuning In To God's Voice In A World Of Static.

JEFF PETHERICK
with KARL NILSSON

Elk Lake
PUBLISHING™

www.elklakepublishing.com • Elk Rapids, Michigan USA

WAVELENGTH

Published by Elk Lake Publishing, Inc.

Copyright ©2007 by Elk Lake Publishing

ISBN-13: 978-0-9793543-0-4

ISBN-10: 0-9793543-0-7

Cover design by Evan Jones
Art direction by Karl Nilsson
Printed in the United States of America

Acknowledgments

God, for your son Jesus, and for pursuing me even when I did not pursue you.

Gina, for loving and supporting me. You are truly God's gift to me.

My children, for loving me and forgiving me for the years I walked without the power of God's truth and love.

My mother and father, who modeled Christ's love even before they knew him, and for their constant prayers.

Craig, who has poured his life into mine, made Jesus real, and kept the flame burning.

Joe, for your friendship and transparency. Thanks for plugging me into community.

My men's group, whose brotherly love and encouragement has deepened my faith.

Steve and Dave, for your obedience to Christ in establishing Kensington Community Church. Your faithfulness and obedience has impacted thousands.

Dave, for your passionate messages that rekindled and stoked the fire.

Karl, for turning my black and white words into Technicolor images.

Contents

"We need to find God, and he cannot be found in noise and restlessness. God is the friend of silence. See how nature – trees, flowers, grass – grows in silence. See how the stars, the moon and the sun move in silence. We need silence to be able to touch souls."

– Mother Teresa

DON'T TOUCH THAT DIAL

Foreword by Karl Nilsson

It never fails. I'm channel surfing through late night cable, looking for something like *I Love Lucy* or *Andy of Mayberry*. But instead of *Mr. Ed*, I come across Mr. Televangelist. And instead of talking to horses, this guy talks to God.

So what is the Creator saying these days? Glad you asked. In the middle of his sermon, the guy with the big hair stops and looks upward. He cocks his head to one side, closes his eyes, and nods a few times to indicate he's receiving a heavenly download. Then he looks directly at me. His gaze goes right through the camera, into my living room, into my heart, and halfway through my La-Z-Boy. This is serious stuff.

The divine revelation he just received is – and I must ask you to sit down for this big surprise – God wants me to send him a donation!

Just about then, my wife walks in. She says God told her I'm supposed to buy her a new dress. And school shoes for the kids. And, oh yeah, the fridge is making funny noises again. So why didn't God tell the TV guy with the limo and the private jet to send *me* some money?

Now this Jeff person says he hears from God, too. But let's not lump him in with the Popeil Pocket Preachers quite yet. In every arena of life there's the counterfeit and there's the genuine article. Jeff's the real deal. In fact, he's so ethical he's practically boring. And unlike the TV preacher, he doesn't wear a shiny suit or use hairspray. Most importantly, he has never once begged anyone (except maybe Santa) to give him a Rolex.

So TV posers aside, let's assume for a moment that someone like Jeff can actually say "God talks to me" and not be a whack job or a con man. Fine. But why call his book about God stuff *Wavelength*?

Here's why: A lot of people think God doesn't speak anymore simply because they've never heard him. Which is like saying China doesn't exist because you've never been there. Or that steak doesn't exist because you've never tasted it.

With that weird logic, you could also conclude that electromagnetic waves don't exist because you can't detect them with your physical senses. *Just like God's voice.* But the instant you turn your radio on, Mariah Carey belting it out is proof that things you can't see, taste, or smell can be very real.

At this moment, hundreds of radio signals are happily beaming through the air whether you know it or not. And radio waves are only the beginning. Unless you live under a Hummer, you're being bombarded with hundreds of undetectable signals from television stations, cell phone towers, short wave operators, and CB radios. With the right gear tuned to the right wavelength, you can access an invisible spectrum of commercial, military, and emergency signals. With a satellite dish, you can sample an endless buffet of video and audio channels. With a police scanner you can listen to cops, firemen, paramedics, pilots, truckers, cabbies, and bug exterminators in action.

Day and night, electromagnetic waves are carrying signals for mobile phones, pagers, garage door openers, walkie-talkies, burglar alarms, remote control toys, cordless telephones, wireless internet, baby monitors, airport radar, global positioning systems, and the key fob to your neighbor's Lexus.

The point is, the transmitters are on, baby. But if you're not tuned in, you will live your life as if the signals don't exist. *Just like God's voice.*

When you push a button and the disc jockey says, "You're listening to 98.5 FM The Rock," what he really means is that you are tuned in to a radio transmitter broadcasting a signal at a precise oscillating frequency of 98.5 million cycles per second. Miss that dial position by a fraction of an inch and all you get is static. Forget to turn the radio on and all you get is silence. Either way, you might conclude that people who claim to hear voices from boxes must be fibbing or delusional or both.

Which is what some folks say about people who claim to hear from God.

Marconi invented the wireless telegraph in 1895. But it was Reginald Fessenden who made the world's first radio broadcast on Christmas Eve, 1906, from Brant Rock, Massachusetts. He played his violin, read from the Bible, and sang a song. Telegraph operators on ships in the Atlantic were shocked to hear a human voice coming from their Morse code equipment. Earlier, when Fessenden asked Thomas Edison if it would ever be possible to transmit voices over radio waves, Edison replied, "Fezzie, what are man's chances of jumping over the moon? I think one is as likely as the other."

Edison was wrong. And so are people who say God no longer speaks to men. As recently as the 1930s, hearing a message from a radio station miles away was a magical experience. Hearing a message from heaven still is.

Getting on God's wavelength is what this book is all about.

1

ORIGINS:
Stirrings of the Heart

You could always spot St. Augustine at the Coliseum.

He was the drunk guy with the giant foam finger, yelling at the gladiator ref, and spilling wine on the row in front of him. What I mean is, before Augustine was a famous saint, he was a famous sinner. Like Bluto in *Animal House*, this guy never missed a toga party. Which is why I identify with him. Not the becoming-a-saint part, but the not-staying-a-frat-boy part.

Anyway, Augie not only invented the soup bowl haircut, he said some really amazing and true things about God like "Thou hast created us for thyself and our heart is not quiet until it rests in thee."

Fifteen centuries later, I came to the same conclusion.

For most of my life, I lived like young Augustine, with a personal philosophy cooked up by my own ego. I had a profitable business, a beautiful family, and a showplace home. I had plenty of friends and a country club membership. In the eyes of the world, I looked successful. But on the inside, I was a basket case and I didn't know why.

At 37, I had already reached every goal I'd set as a young man, but I didn't feel fulfilled. I looked around and wondered what it would take to satisfy my hunger for inner peace and happiness. Friends jokingly suggested the usual antidotes for mid-life crisis – a sports car, a mistress, a junket to Vegas. Thankfully, I didn't look to Caesar's Palace, a Corvette, or a leggy blond for answers. I started to look to God.

Or should I say *listen*.

That's right. I know it sounds weird, but I'm pretty sure God was speaking to me way back then. And despite the fact I had no real relationship with him, I was somehow hearing his voice. Acting on his leading, I moved my family to the peace and tranquility of a country home, and in the beauty of nature, our lives began to be transformed.

Eventually, God led us to a new kind of church with an old kind of message. For the first time, we heard that we could have a deep and personal relationship with Jesus Christ.

In time, we stepped into that relationship, and our spiritual journey hit overdrive. The peace, love, and joy perks that Jesus promised poured into our lives. Don't get me wrong. We didn't lose our bad habits or drop our emotional baggage overnight. Nor did we live in some kind of heavenly rose garden. We still worried, yelled, bickered, complained and judged. But real changes did take place, and we began to experience major blessings in our family.

I'm a skeptic by nature. So early on I decided to investigate this whole "God thing" by reading and analyzing deep books by deep authors. Theological heavyweights replaced *Forbes* and *Barrons* on my coffee table. You could say I gave Jesus my "head" – rooting my faith in archaeological evidence and historical facts about the flesh-and-blood carpenter. But while it provided an intellectual foundation, human reason alone could not sustain me in the long term.

It wasn't until I gave Jesus my *heart* that I truly tasted what's called the "fruit of the Spirit" (peace, patience, kindness, self control, etc. from Galatians 5:22). The stories in this book describe some of the spiritual fruit I've munched on since coming to know God more intimately.

Back in college, I loved to write. Poems, stories, grocery lists – writing provided a welcome creative outlet. But when I jumped into the fast lane of chasing money and success, things I loved to do fell by the wayside. Since then, I've often toyed with the idea of writing a book. I even started to pen an adventure novel, but I kept dozing off (a really, really bad sign). Crime, sports, westerns – I just didn't have enough "burn" about any one subject to finish a book.

Until I met Jesus.

As one spiritual encounter after another occurred in my life, I hurriedly recorded the events on paper. One day, while re-reading my journal, I felt prompted by God to compile these stories in a book.

Jeff's peanut brain: *Why me? I'm a Chartered Financial Analyst. My bag is numbers, not theology.*

God's infinite wisdom: *Bookstores are bulging with books written by professional clergy, but there are darn few by ordinary laymen who've experienced me in profound ways. Kapish?*

Oh, yeah, I understood. Like many of us, I grew up with the religious mindset that only ordained ministers or priests could truly experience God in their lives. I was taught it was these chosen few who "talked" with God. They, in turn, would pass their findings on to sinners like me whose communication line to God was broken or full of static.

At Kensington Community Church in Troy, Michigan, I heard a much different approach. The pastors there freely and publicly admitted their sins. Their weaknesses and failures were evidently as great as mine. But they had one thing I did not – the reality of Jesus Christ in their lives. After hearing them speak so candidly about their feet of clay, I became passionate to know more about their redeemer: *Who was he? How did he live? What promises did he make?*

Soon I learned that Jesus not only loved me in some huge cosmic sense, but was interested in me personally. When he died and ascended into heaven, he sent his Holy Spirit to guide me in this earthly life. By worshiping, praying, and meditating on Scripture, my hotline to God was repaired, and our day-to-day relationship grew stronger. As I came closer to God, he came closer to me (James 4:8).

Since my spiritual rebirth, God has been pulling me into the lives of others through letters, phone calls, and unusual "coincidences." The stories are messy, some don't have happy endings, and most are still works in progress. I'm not sure what God has in store for my future, so I concentrate on living deeply dependent and fully aware in the present. Instead of plotting my own course of action, I'm trying to follow his plan and respond whenever I feel his Spirit stirring in my heart.

These are the true, unvarnished accounts of how God has done extraordinary things through the life of one very ordinary man.

2

ROADBLOCKS:
Thick As A Brick

Albert Einstein defined insanity as "Doing the same thing over and over and expecting different results."

By that definition, we were insane.

It wasn't rocket science, but it took us a long time to finally get it. To be sure, God had tried many times to get our attention. But maybe we were just too stubborn. Or thick-headed. In any case, my wife and I thought we were doing the right things: going to church, donating to charity, and volunteering in our community.

But truthfully, we were just trying to pump up our heavenly resumes. My plan was to show up at the pearly gates, high-five St. Peter and hand him my list of accomplishments. No doubt Pete would be impressed by my glowing report card. If heaven graded on a curve, I was a shoe-in.

Thankfully, the Lord had a different plan. He graciously (but firmly) revealed he was not all that impressed by my good deeds. When God held up his mirror to my life, I saw a self-absorbed man living a selfish life in his own way on his own terms for his own benefit.

Ouch.

Somebody once called Frank Sinatra's *I Did It My Way* the theme song of hell. I'm not sure if it made the Fire & Brimstone Top Ten, but the narcissistic lyrics described my lifestyle perfectly.

The only times I asked God (or anyone else) for advice was when I was scared, sick, or broke. Outside of my 9-1-1 rescue prayers, I pretty much ignored him. The idea of turning my life over to him was nowhere on my radar screen. But God has a way of working in our lives – even when we don't acknowledge him. And that's exactly what he was doing. While I was still clueless about his will, he was quietly moving behind the scenes. All I knew was that changes were taking place.

It would be many years before I recognized God's hand in it all...

o   o   o

Gina and I met in high school at a party. She had been drinking and needed someone to help her get some fresh air. Luckily, I happened to be standing in the street when she wandered out with a friend. We connected immediately. Despite the unusual circumstance of our first encounter, I sensed there was something special about her, and I wanted to know her better. Much better. Fortunately for our future offspring, she called the next day to thank me for helping.

We talked for hours.

For some reason, I knew early on that I would marry her. I felt a mysterious "divine hand" on our relationship from day one. So did Gina. She used to say that her mother was looking down from heaven and brought me into her life to protect her. When Gina was a second-grader, her mom was killed by a drunk driver. At about the same time, my older brother was disrupting my family with his own substance abuse.

Having seen the ugly effects of booze and drugs first-hand, Gina and I agreed our group of intoxicated friends was a bad influence. We both wanted to do something more meaningful with our lives than drinking and vomiting, so we began spending more time with each other and less with the party crowd. As we searched for deeper meaning in the backseat of my dad's Chevy Malibu, friendship blossomed into love and we dated hot and heavy through high school.

While I went away to Albion College, Gina stayed home, worked, and attended night school. We stuck together and were married shortly after my graduation. Three years later our son Chad was born, and two years after that we had a daughter, Kira.

At the time I became a father, I was a "spiritual" person and believed in God. Sort of. I even conceded that Jesus might be the Son of God, but never thought about the implications. My advanced theology was: *If I do the best I can, pay my taxes, and don't hurt anyone, everything in life will work out just fine.*

Sorry, wrong answer. Next contestant, please.

At first, both our babies seemed normal and healthy. Ten toes, good Apgar, big sigh of relief. But shortly after Kira's birth, we knew something was wrong: She never stopped crying. Literally. It was non-stop from the time she woke up until the time she went to bed. The doctors said it was colic, a mysterious ailment of the digestive system. They said she would grow out of it, but for five months it was emotional hell.

I would return from work at 6:30 p.m. to spend a half-hour with Gina before she fell into bed from sheer exhaustion. I would spend the next four hours walking in a circle with Kira cradled across my stomach. In desperation, I pleaded with God to quiet her. As I paced, I cycled through a dizzying range of emotions. Each night I would shift from incredible pity for this innocent angel who could not be comforted to incredible anger at this demon baby who would not stop crying. Adding to the misery, I capped off every evening with a good shot of stomach-churning guilt for being so upset at my helpless daughter's condition.

As parents, we wanted to offer Kira the love and nurturing she deserved, but it took all of our energy just to endure the noise. More than once I asked God, "What did I do to deserve this punishment?" Whatever reservoir of patience I had (and it wasn't much to begin with) ran dry each night as Kira screamed. Gina's patience (though greater than mine) was stretched to the breaking point.

Kira's high decibel tirades were by far the toughest challenge of our marriage. Beyond the impact on our own sanity, we worried about Kira's future. Because the first six months are so critical to a child's development, I was secretly afraid of long-term damage and personality disorders.

I hoped I was wrong, but my fears proved to be correct.

Starting in the second grade, we had frequent meetings with Kira's teachers about her disruptive behavior. She would have loud emotional outbursts in class and it would take her hours to calm down. We had her tested numerous times, but each expert said she was normal or that she would outgrow the problem.

When Kira was seven, we left the affluent suburb we'd been raised in and moved to the country. Both Gina and I were troubled that the old-fashioned values of our hometown were shifting with the increased prosperity. Over two cups of $6 latte (kidding), we decided it wasn't where we wanted to raise our kids. On top of that, my job as portfolio manager for a Boston-based money management firm had become increasingly stressful. A nature boy at heart, I needed some elbow room where I could unwind.

Packing up the moving van, we headed for the wide open spaces – despite dire warnings from our city-slicker parents and friends. It seemed like a great move for Gina and me, but even more so for Kira who would benefit from a fresh start with new friends and teachers. I now believe God orchestrated this *Green Acres* relocation primarily so we would slow down enough to hear him speaking to us.

That fall, we enrolled our kids in an elite private school. During the admission interview, I had an uneasy feeling. The headmaster of 28 years was retiring and moving away. A young, career-minded man had been hired to replace him, and I knew in my gut it was a bad fit. Kira's behavior issues did not subside, and after the first semester we were called into the headmaster's office.

Remember Mr. Freeze from *Batman*? This guy was colder. In a calm voice, he told us matter-of-factly that if Kira's behavior did not improve in the second semester, she would be asked not to return. It was clear this new executive wanted no problem students to stain his budding career, especially in his first year at a prestigious school.

Gina and I were stunned by his lack of sympathy. Nothing wounds a parent's heart more deeply than indifference toward their struggling child. At the end of the year, we pulled both kids from the school and enrolled them in the local public elementary.

In her first year at this new school, Kira's behavior issues surfaced again. Frustrated teachers called almost daily. It tore Gina apart to hear the phone ring, and we tried everything humanly possible to help the situation. While our faith in the "man upstairs" wasn't much to begin with, it grew weaker by the day. We were angry at God, and openly questioned his actions and motives.

Luckily, God has thick skin.

Unknown to us then, he was quite aware of what was happening and *why* it was happening. Most of all, he knew we would soon be turning to him for answers.

In December, Gina was invited to a ladies' brunch sponsored by Kensington Community Church. The keynote speaker was Nancy Holcomb, the sister of the church's senior pastor, Steve Andrews. The mother of six, she described how her third son, Jay, was born with spina bifida. Jay was not expected to live 14 days, but against all odds, he lived nearly 14 years. Despite having 11 major surgeries, Jay's courage and optimism inspired his parents, siblings, and neighbors. By the end of his life, he had touched the lives of thousands in his Memphis community.

This gripping account of one family's unconditional love for a special needs child opened Gina's eyes to a whole new possibility.

Returning home, she called me in tears. "How can we be so consumed by our daughter's struggles?" she sobbed. "Kira is physically healthy now and will be emotionally healthy someday. We need to just trust God that he will make her better. Besides, our problem pales in comparison to Nancy's, and her faith in God was not destroyed by her experience, but strengthened."

Before hanging up, we resolved that once the New Year began we would check out this new and unknown church.

Frankly, I was a bit nervous.

Loading up the kids, we drove to Kensington with mixed emotions: Gina worried about her shoes matching her purse, I worried about having to drink the grape Kool-Aid. I was relieved when we were welcomed by nice non-psycho people who had never heard of Jim Jones and couldn't care less about how we dressed. During our first service they showed a video about a couple named Lori and Steve who had been struggling in their marriage. Fed up with fighting, Lori had begun attending a Bible study and it was changing her life. She tried to convey this to her husband, but he wouldn't listen. Eventually, however, Steve was invited to a men's group, and his life also began to change. His heart softened and for some reason he started playing his guitar again for the first time since college.

As the video ended, a single beam of light shone down to illuminate a solitary figure on stage. It was Steve from the video, seated on a stool with a guitar in his hands. Softly, he began to sing a love song he had written to his wife and to God. Choking back tears, he barely made it through the final verses. As the lights came up in the auditorium, I could see that hundreds of people had been deeply moved by this testimony.

At the end of the service, Kira looked at me with tears in her eyes and said, "Daddy, do we have to go back to our old church?" Then my son Chad said, "Dad, there is something about this place. It touches me right here," and pointed to his heart. I nearly fell over. I looked at my family and declared, "I think we have found our home."

That was the good news. The bad news was that Gina and I were soon at our wits' end again. We consulted every doctor we could find, but nothing was working. In fact, the situation was getting worse: Kira frequently talked about hurting herself and her self-esteem was lower than ever.

We were a family on the verge of meltdown.

One evening in March, Gina and I were lying in bed, arguing (as usual) about what to do with Kira. I was bitter and confused and angry that her behavior was not improving – as if she could control whatever was afflicting her. Compared to me, Gina was a rock. She would not give up, no matter what it might take to make our daughter emotionally healthy. But despite my wife's unswerving commitment, we were drowning in the worst pain we'd ever experienced.

Tears running down our faces, we held hands and agreed it was finally time to give up control to God. Our plan was not working. We needed his plan. Desperately. One at a time, we prayed out loud to God, surrendering to his will and asking him into our lives. As the words left my lips, burdens and heartaches I had stored up for years seemed to lift off my shoulders. I looked at Gina and asked if she too felt the release. Eyes brimming with tears of joy, she nodded "yes."

We felt as light as feathers floating on a breeze.

I looked at my beautiful wife and said, "I can't believe it. What we heard at Kensington is true. God is real and he cares deeply for us. He has just been patiently waiting for us to figure that out." We cried together for what seemed like hours, caught up in the love of Jesus, and comforted in the knowledge that somehow, things were going to be all right.

Shortly after asking Jesus into our lives, answers for Kira began to come. Gina "just happened" to be watching *Oprah* one afternoon when the topic was childhood depression. Noticing the symptoms seemed to match Kira's, she bought the recommended book called *Lonely, Sad and Angry* by Dr. Ingersoll and Dr. Goldstein. Since depression ran in my family, Gina guessed she might be on the right track.

At the same time, Kira "coincidentally" got a new elementary school principal – one who was compassionate and eager to help us. She recommended we see Dr. Steve Schlabach, a local physician specializing in depression, especially in young children. After giving Kira a number of tests, he concluded she was severely depressed.

Dr. Steve explained to us that, unlike adults, depressed children tend to be angry and defiant, often acting out with strong emotional outbursts. He was describing Kira's behavior perfectly. For the first time, we were getting real answers.

Kira's prognosis changed from a hopeless mystery to a treatable condition overnight. Overnight! We were thrilled. As brand new believers, we chalked our reversal of fortune to luck or coincidence. But the longer we followed Jesus, the more we saw clear evidence of an invisible God working behind the scenes. For us, the unexplainable synchronicity pointed to some grand design.

As we searched for *spiritual* health, our daughter's *emotional* health improved. With help from totally unexpected sources, Kira finally got the treatment she needed. After years of struggling, she soon blossomed into a beautiful young lady who felt confident and comfortable about herself. She went on to dance competitively, join the cheerleading team, and travel on mission trips. She knows that God used a wonderful doctor and modern medicines to help her, but she also knows that Jesus was – and is – the ultimate healer in her life.

When Kira had her breakthrough, I was just a wet-behind-the-ears rookie but I knew this much for sure: God was real, he was big, and he worked through people.

I also knew that I wanted to be one of those people he worked through. But before I could report for duty, I needed to get a few things straight with my new boss.

For me, asking Jesus to be the master or CEO of my life was the beginning of a long process. Since that very first night when Gina and I experienced the incredible feeling of weightlessness, I was hooked on Jesus. But even though my *heart* belonged to God, my *head* was not fully convinced.

To better understand who Jesus was, I read dozens of books about the historical accuracy of the Bible. I devoured newer books like *The Case for Christ* by Lee Strobel. I studied classics like *Evidence That Demands A Verdict* by Josh McDowell.

I listened to messages by Bill Hybels about a loving Creator who sent his Son to earth. Gradually, I became intellectually convinced that Jesus was who he said he was.

For a time, it seemed the pendulum had swung too far: My *head* was now convinced but my *heart* was less engaged. Fortunately, the love affair that began at my conversion soon came back full circle. I realized that to experience the amazing power of Jesus in my life, he must have control of my heart. To truly surrender meant to not just acknowledge God's existence, but to let *his* will become *my* will.

That was the metaphysical bridge from the mundane to the miraculous.

Once I got this through my fat cranium, I began to experience Jesus working in my life in exciting ways. God began stirring in my heart. Prayer became a two-way conversation. He spoke, I obeyed, and the stories came tumbling out, one after another.

○   ○   ○

"I keep asking that God… may give you the Spirit of wisdom and revelation, so that you may know him better. I pray also that the eyes of your heart may be enlightened in order that you may know the hope to which he has called you, the riches of his glorious inheritance in the saints, and his incomparably great power for us who believe." (Ephesians 1:17-19)

3

PRIDE:
Conditional Surrender

It had to be quick, painless, and foolproof. But most of all, Joe's death had to look like an accident. If investigators suspected suicide, his family would never see a penny of life insurance.

With calm precision, he stopped his car, unbuckled his seatbelt, and stepped onto the gravel shoulder. Inches away, cars and trucks roared by at 50 miles per hour. Inside Joe's head, images of family competed with agonizing pain for his attention. Just a few more seconds and the struggle that had been raging for 12 months would finally be over. No more nightmares. No more shame. No more running from God…

○   ○   ○

I first met Joe because I like to sing in the shower. Most men do. And for a lot of us, that's the best place for our crooning. But after years of using soap-on-a-rope as my microphone, I decided to take the plunge and audition for the church choir.

I'd been a believer for just under a year and I was feeling ready to get more involved at my church. We'd been learning about the importance of community to the Christian life, but as newcomers we didn't know how to get connected. Since I had performed in musicals as a kid, I decided to try out for the chorale. By some kind of miracle, I passed the audition, got a huge recording contract, and toured the country in a custom bus. Okay, I made up the last part, but for me, the idea of teaming up with 50 singers onstage was an incredible thrill.

At my first rehearsal, I met Joe and we quickly became friends. I liked his sense of humor and quick wit, but what really drew me to Joe was his godly wisdom. He'd been following Jesus a lot longer than me, and there was something strong and determined about him that I wanted to emulate. Between songs, the likable baritone explained that he was trying to live "differently from the world's way," and perhaps I should, too.

Kensington Community Church was celebrating its 10th anniversary that March. To mark the occasion, the chorale performed at seven services over two days. During that long weekend, Joe and I spent a lot of backstage time together and ventured way beyond surface conversations. After one service, I shared how coming to Kensington had stirred something in my heart. I told him I'd never had such a passion to learn about Jesus. I asked if he knew a men's group I could join to study the Bible.

Joe blinked hard. His eyes grew wide. He looked pale, then flushed. For an instant I wondered if I'd somehow offended him or said something wrong. Regaining composure, Joe said, "I've been feeling for a long time now that I should start a men's group, but I never followed through with it. You just confirmed that God wants me to stop stalling."

In that instant I understood how Jesus can move deeply

and privately in one person's heart and then use *another* person to nudge them past their indecision. Obviously, God had already been working on Joe, and I was thrilled that he used my question to push him over the edge. For the first time I realized that macro-God could use micro-me to help accomplish his will.

Within a month, Joe's new group was meeting every Tuesday at noon. Most of us worked in the area and it was a convenient time that didn't yank us away from our families. The first book we studied was the New Testament epistle of James. It's short, but power-packed with prescriptions for spiritual health.

Some of us were new in our faith, others more experienced. But from babes to veterans, we had all found ourselves drifting, and yearned for fellowship and direction. The study was rich and conversations flowed easily with a mix of youthful enthusiasm and seasoned perspective.

As we grew to trust each other, Joe eventually let down his guard enough to share the troubling story behind his confident facade. Turns out I was right in my first impression – Joe did have plenty of Bible knowledge and tons of valuable experience. And there was no doubt he was trying his best to live a godly life. But I was beginning to find a huge disconnect between the knowledge in Joe's head and the actions in Joe's life.

Like many of us, Joe struggled in applying God's truth to everyday living. Despite his knowledge of scripture, he had plenty of doubts. Underneath a cheery exterior, he was discouraged and fearful that God could not (or would not) forgive him for his mistakes. Bit by bit, he reluctantly opened up to me, and I began to see the real reasons for his anguish.

In an earlier career, Joe had been an accountant for a private company. By working hard, he was eventually promoted to controller. He described the euphoria of hitting the top rung in the corporate ladder: great salary, great perks, and all the trappings of success. From Joe's perspective, he would be "set for life financially". The here-and-now was good, and the future looked even better.

Two weeks after starting his new position, tragedy struck.

The day of Joe's family picnic was sunny and only a few fluffy clouds dotted the July sky. Surrounded by the people he loved most, he cracked jokes and grilled his signature spareribs. After lunch, he promised his sister he would watch her young daughter so she could take a short break from supervising the energetic toddler.

A good uncle, Joe watched his niece carefully, but for a brief moment he became distracted in conversation. When he turned around, the 2-year-old girl was missing. Within moments, the peaceful family gathering erupted into a full-blown panic. Adults and kids frantically searched the campground. Running hard, out of breath, Joe and his sister raced to the water's edge only to find the lifeless child floating face down in the Muskegon River.

Joe scooped up the limp body and rushed back to the picnic area as someone dialed 9-1-1. He gave the little girl mouth-to-mouth resuscitation for what seemed like an eternity. When the emergency team finally arrived, they raced her to an area hospital. To everyone's relief, doctors were successful in reviving Joe's niece. Unfortunately, oxygen deprivation to the brain had caused permanent damage and she would never be the same.

Neither would Joe.

He fell into a deep depression. His career and personal life began to unravel. While his sister never blamed Joe for the accident, he could not forgive himself. For months after the incident, he walked around in a daze. Friends noticed a profound change, but strangely no one intervened or tried to help. Even the minister at the Episcopal church where Joe served as an elder ignored the problem.

This neglect confirmed Joe's impression that no one loved him or cared about him. *Why should they?* he thought, *I'm the one that let my niece drown that day.* Racked with guilt, Joe decided his life wasn't worth much and the world would be better off without him. He decided to end his life.

To keep his wife and two small children from suffering financially, Joe concocted a scheme to embezzle money from his employers. With a big enough chunk of cash in the bank, his widow could pay off the mortgage and continue living in a nice neighborhood. He set up a dummy corporate account, and quickly funneled $50,000 into it. He intended to siphon off much more, but his company fired him in the midst of the scam – for an entirely different reason.

After the accident, the owners of Joe's firm were sympathetic to his mood swings, but as months dragged on they grew impatient with his poor job performance. As his depression deepened, his work suffered. Finally they were forced to replace him.

Shortly after being fired, Joe received a chilling phone call from the company: They suspected a large sum of money was missing. He knew his theft had been uncovered. The impending investigation and prosecution kicked his suicide plan into high gear.

Driving along a narrow stretch of western Michigan highway, Joe figured out a way to die that would look like an accident. He pulled his green Ford Taurus to the side of the road and let the air out of the left front tire. Then he jacked up the car, removed the five lug nuts and pulled the flat tire off. Clutching the heavy wheel, he braced himself to fall backwards into oncoming traffic and certain death.

Up to this point, the thought of his self-execution never

fazed him. He believed a staged accident was his only option and was fully bent on his own destruction. But as he squatted on the dusty roadside, images of his beautiful children came streaming into his consciousness. Joe swears he felt the Lord's presence that hot summer evening in a tangible and powerful way. Seconds before pitching himself into oncoming traffic, he heard the words in his mind, *"You cannot do this. It's not your life to take."*

Trembling with fear, he cried out to God, "Then what am I going to do with my life?" Immediately, a feeling of peace flooded over him as he realized he was getting a second chance. He knew there would still be a heavy price to pay. But he also knew he was feeling God's unconditional love for the first time in his life. Overwhelmed, he collapsed to the shoulder of the road and sobbed uncontrollably.

Joe had always been a God-fearing man, but he didn't understand the concept of a personal relationship with Jesus. He was dutifully, mechanically going through the motions of a religious life. Yet despite his plan to commit a "cardinal sin", here was God, personally with him on the side of the road like heaven's own AAA.

Suddenly, life seemed worth living.

Joe put the spare tire on and drove off with the firm conviction that whatever good or bad came down life's highway, he would never again have to face it alone. And while his conviction for embezzlement was followed by a painful divorce, the seeds of healing planted on Highway 31 refused to die.

He began attending Kensington where he soon met the woman who would become his second wife. Together with her three children and two of his own, Joe strived to be the family man he had always wanted to be. But as any stepfather will tell you, the tensions of leading a blended family are enormous. By the time Joe began his men's group, he was stressed out from the pressure of trying to be a good husband, father, and breadwinner.

For a time, Joe was able to easily provide for his family with his own financial software business. But when technology shifted, he was caught unprepared. His business suffered. He tried to get a steady job, but whenever a company got close to hiring him, his criminal record blocked the deal.

When bad times hit, they can make us better or bitter. Joe picked bitter. Instead of being grateful that God was supernaturally sustaining him through his unemployment, he was envious and angry that other people around him seemed to be prospering.

In addition to his money problems, Joe had issues with his stepchildren, and was hurt by their seeming lack of respect. With constant conflict in the household and a deteriorating financial situation, his marriage began to suffer.

Outwardly, Joe still gave the impression that he followed the Bible. But inside, he was unable to fully accept Jesus' forgiveness. He was a guilt-ridden man who felt he did not deserve anyone's love – especially God's. Old behaviors kept resurfacing and bad habits seemed impossible to kick.

Joe looked at his rough circumstances and concluded he was being divinely punished. He was convinced God was tormenting him for past mistakes, and wondered how long he would have to suffer. Maybe he would lose everything he treasured like the Old Testament patriarch Job. Or maybe the Lord would make him wander in the desert like Moses. Worst of all, Joe wasn't sure if his wilderness experience would last 40 days or 40 years.

All he knew was that his past continued to haunt him.

A surprising breakthrough came when Joe had our group tackle the classic study *Experiencing God* by Henry Blackaby.

During that course, Joe began to see the amazing things God had done for him and to sense the reality of Jesus in his life.

The study illuminated another important truth. For years, Joe had been asking himself, "Why did God spare my life that night? What is the one unique thing he wants me to do?" He felt that if he could just answer that pivotal question, he would be freed from the torment of his past.

The answer eluded him until he realized the right question was not "What is God's *specific* will for *my* life?", but rather, "What is God's *general* will for *everybody's* life?" In Blackaby's book, Joe saw that God has a primary will that applies to all of mankind. He saw that step one of God's universal plan is for each of us to know and understand him: *"So that you may know and believe me and understand that I am he"* (Isaiah 43:10).

This first, basic step of knowing God is critical, because the more we know him, the more we love him. And the more we love him, the easier it is to surrender our will to him. Once we are obeying his *general* will, then – and only then – God can use us to perform his *specific* will.

That October, I took Joe and several men from Kensington up to a remote cabin in northern Michigan for some grouse hunting. The weather was crisp. The unpolluted skies were azure and the colors of the changing leaves were spectacular. Each night we'd gather around the fireplace to talk about the hunt, the beauty of nature, and what century the Detroit Lions might win the Super Bowl.

After dinner one evening, I asked the group how they had experienced God working in their life during the past year. Joe was the last to speak, and he was choked with emotion. He shared that even after becoming a Christian he didn't truly believe God loved him. Tearfully, he explained how he had only recently accepted the idea that Jesus was not judging him for past mistakes. No matter how badly he screwed up, Jesus saw Joe as a sinless person, set free from the gravitational pull of his past. As the fire's last embers faded, Joe confided that he had finally begun to live his life according to God's will.

After the hunt, Joe's heart began to change from ungratefulness to thankfulness. He no longer saw himself being punished, but being blessed. For the first time, he submitted to the Lord – not merely with lip service, but by humbling himself and accepting God's gift of grace.

It seemed as if Joe's walk in the desert was coming to an end.

In December, he was hired as a supervisor at a Big Three automotive plant. While it wasn't the dream job Joe was hoping for, the guys in our men's group told him to grab it and see where God would lead.

Joe took our advice and worked hard that year, often putting in 70-hour weeks. The money paid off the bills, but the grueling hours and harsh factory environment took their toll. When management asked him to switch to another shift that would take him away from his family, he declined the transfer. He took the ultimatum as a sign that God wanted him to move on. Certainly another opportunity would come along that matched his qualifications better. After all, he deserved it.

Or so he thought.

When no jobs came, his attitude soured. Like Joe, most of us will always struggle with whatever original weakness deterred us from embracing Jesus in the first place. For me, it's "control." For others it's fear, or greed, or maybe a toxic religious background. For Joe, it was the one area all of us are tempted in – *pride*.

Our pride is easily wounded by things like lack of respect from our children, lack of appreciation from our spouse, or lack of recognition in our careers. Joe was slammed by all three at once in a perfect storm of rejection.

The only way Joe (or anyone else) can survive rejection is to replace the source of our self-image. When we derive our self-esteem from the unchanging God who loves us unconditionally, we're less susceptible to the roller coaster circumstances of life (layoffs, promotions, illness, etc.) and other people's opinions (criticisms, flattery, gossip, etc.).

While Joe's job loss could have been a powerful lesson in humility, it didn't sink in. Instead of blaming his pride, he blamed God. Instead of having a positive attitude, he stubbornly hung onto negative junk like an emotional pack rat – allowing failures, struggles, and pain to dominate his thoughts.

With Joe's heart divided and vulnerable, Satan poured in his lies: *You're too rotten to be forgiven. How could anyone love you that much?* Like a cancer, these doubts metastasized and crowded out the truth. When the assurance of God's love and forgiveness is replaced by lies, our weakest areas – like pride – always come back to haunt us.

It's not in the dictionary, but a good definition of pride is "being a do-it-yourselfer." By trying to do things on his own, Joe was implying that success or failure rested on his shoulders. By taking matters into his own hands, Joe was saying "no thanks" to God's free offer to be his helper, forgiver, counselor, and manager.

Pride tricks us into believing that we can get ahead, solve problems, or change behavior by our own efforts. But the old saying "God helps those who help themselves" is not to be found in the Bible.

In fact, the opposite is true. Jesus said, *"Apart from me you can do nothing"* (John 15:5). It's his power – not ours – that we are to rely on: *"I can do everything through him who gives me strength"* (Philippians 4:13).

After watching Joe vacillate between self-love and self-loathing, I had an epiphany: What seems arbitrary about how and when God chooses to "bless us" largely depends on – drum roll, please – our response to whatever he asks us to do.

If God puts us in the hot dry desert, it's for good reasons that only he can know. But if we trust him, we can rest assured the desert is exactly where we need to be. Obviously, God was asking a lot from Joe, and to this day, my friend is leaning hard on Jesus to get him through. I pray that he will keep himself in a position to hear God's voice, and that he will respond to it promptly without dragging his feet.

Why is quickness important? Because there is no predetermined length of time we have to spend "wandering in the desert." Whether we learn fast or slow is up to us. Whether we obey cheerfully (with humility) or grudgingly (with pride) is up to us. But either way – tortoise or hare – the race isn't over until we reach the point of brokenness where God can reassemble our shattered pieces into a masterpiece built in his image.

When and if any of us will be "lifted up" is simply a matter of how long it takes us to humble ourselves and be broken before God: *"Humble yourselves, therefore, under God's mighty hand, that he may lift you up in due time"* (1 Peter 5:6).

4

PRAYER:
Enlarging My Territory

Which would be worse? Being shot or being stabbed?

Images of my body sprawled out on the pavement raced through my mind. *Should I turn and run or strike the first blow? Is this man blocking my path a common thief or a desperate drug addict?* All I knew was that something very bad was going down and I was the victim. Sweat trickled down my face as I looked into the vacant eyes of a man who could end my life for a hit of crack...

Bookstores, drugstores, supermarkets – everywhere you turned, the *Prayer of Jabez* was being sold. As sales soared into the millions, public interest hit a fever pitch in 2001. Soon after our men's group began the Bruce Wilkinson study on marriage, the topic of his bestseller *Jabez* came up. I liked the book's simple message, and it spurred my interest in developing a life of prayer.

I'll be honest. Praying was not something that came naturally to me, and I believed I had to pray the "right" way before God would listen to me. Little did I know he doesn't care so much about *how* we pray but *why*. What's most important is not our style but our motive: Do we look to God in utter dependence or do we rattle off a shopping list for him to fill?

Misguided or not, my early prayers were nonetheless enthusiastic, and I always finished by quoting the prayer of Jabez: *"Oh, that you would bless me indeed and enlarge my territory, that your hand would be with me, and that you would keep me from evil so that I may not cause pain"* (1 Chronicles 4:10).

While reading Wilkinson's book, I was called by a consultant to make a presentation to one of their clients in Buffalo, New York. They were looking for an investment manager, and our style of investing fit their needs. The deal was lucrative, but it was going to be a tough sell. We'd experienced little success with this particular consultant, and two other top firms would be competing for the business.

Tough or not, this was an ideal opportunity to show the consultant what our newly formed team could do for her clients. Just a year earlier, a group of us had left the comfort and stability of a large investment firm to start our own business. The Buffalo pitch would be a chance for our young financial management group to break into the big leagues.

Because the meeting was early in the morning, I flew out the night before to Buffalo. I stayed at a hotel that was fairly close to the meeting which was to be held at a private club in downtown Buffalo. I brought *The Prayer of Jabez* with me, and finished it that evening before going to bed.

Next morning, I awoke with the typical jitters I get before every major presentation. But because of the book, I was now in the habit of praying every morning. Before going down for breakfast, I asked Jesus for his guidance and peace during my presentation so I could honor him in the process. And, of course, so that we could win the business.

As always, I finished with the prayer of Jabez.

I walked out of the hotel with confidence and looked for a taxi. But Buffalo is not Manhattan and there were no cabs in sight. I thought the meeting was just around the corner and down a few blocks so I decided to walk. As I walked, I daydreamed about enlarging my territory: *We don't have any clients in Buffalo, so this would certainly be a fitting way to expand our reach.*

And why not? Didn't Bruce Wilkinson say we should ask for more territory so our sphere of influence for God's glory would be expanded? Sounded good to me. Real good. But when my conscience kicked in I began to question my motives: *Did I want this huge chunk of business for God or for myself?* I guessed that I wanted it more for my pocketbook and my pride than anything altruistic.

I tried to convince God otherwise, but he wasn't buying it.

Deep in thought and now disturbed by my mixed motives, I walked on. Suddenly, I realized that while I was walking and thinking I had strayed into a dangerous part of town. Iron security bars on the windows and doors told me this was a much tougher neighborhood than I was used to. Dressed in a perfectly tailored business suit and carrying a leather briefcase, I was a fish out of water. Way out. Shabbily dressed men and teens in gang colors milled around boarded-up buildings and abandoned cars.

I tried not to act nervous, but I could literally feel the stares of everyone around me. Maybe it was just curiosity about why I was on foot in such a high risk area. Or maybe it was anger or even pity. Whatever their actual intent, I felt like somebody was going to try a move on me at any second.

Just when it seemed like I was headed for trouble, I crossed a street and suddenly there were trees and flowers and nicely maintained buildings. One block more, and I was back in the nicer part of town and at the doorstep of the exclusive club.

I was the first presenter that morning and the board was ready for me right away. After brief introductions, I started into my presentation. About a third of the way into it, one of the trustees asked a very academic and technical question. I had no trouble answering it, but I was surprised at how quickly this man had tried to knock me off my presentation by pulling out the "tough" question. As soon as I finished my answer, he looked at me without emotion, gathered up his papers and left the room.

It got worse. As he exited, two other trustees got up from the board table and also walked out. Watching the other two leave, I wondered if I had said something to offend them. I had never seen this kind of disrespect before, let alone experienced it. Trustees just don't leave in the middle of a presentation.

I was stunned and began to lose my train of thought. I mumbled something and paused to regain my composure. I was mad – no, make that mad as hell – and I wanted to tell the remaining group that I had never been treated so rudely. My pride was wounded, and the only thing I could think of was to repay the insult. With interest. Then, during this pause, I felt the presence and peace of Jesus wash over me. It was exactly what I had prayed for earlier. I regained my composure, took a deep breath and finished the presentation. My renewed efforts were greeted by silence.

I was devastated.

As I left the building, I was consumed by how poorly the presentation had gone. After crashing and burning like the Hindenburg, there was no way we were ever going to win the business. Replays of the men walking out and me going brain-dead went through my mind like a bad movie.

Once again, I was deep in thought, with my body on autopilot heading back to the hotel. And once again, I inadvertently wandered into the same bad part of town. This time, however, the sidewalks were lined with young men, looking tough with their baggy pants worn low and cinched around their hips. Despite the sweltering heat, they wore hooded sweatshirts with caps pulled down over their heads. Chalking up my earlier safe passage to beginner's luck, I calculated I wouldn't make it through this gauntlet without being confronted, mugged, or worse.

Trying to look brave, I made my way past tenements covered in graffiti. Out of the corner of my eye, I noticed a young man standing in the shadows, leaning up against a building. Before I could pass, he stepped out of the darkness and came straight for me. Believe me, I know my rights and I had every right to be scared to death. But unlike my earlier encounter, I had a peace about me and was certain I heard Jesus whisper, *Don't worry. He isn't going to hurt you.*

Built like a prize fighter, the man stopped me cold. I dodged left, then right, but he straddled the sidewalk like a human roadblock and there was no getting past. He looked like a gang member and I was sure he had a gun tucked in his waist. He pushed up to within inches of my face and blurted out "Man, I got to tell you the truth!"

He reeked of alcohol. As I backed away from his hot breath, I looked at him with a calm assurance that should not have been and said, "Yeah, what's that?"

Eyes widening, he yelled, "Man, I got to tell you the truth! I know I smell like booze, 'cuz I been drinking all night, but you gotta trust me, man. I ain't gonna lie to you. My mother lives in Albany and she is really sick, man. I need some money for bus fare to go up and see her."

Of course I figured this was the sucker line of the day to

get money for Jack Daniels and smokes. But something told me to keep talking to this man. It seemed like God controlled my tongue as I heard myself ask him his name. He replied "Rodney."

I said, "Rodney, let me ask you a big question. Do you know God?"

Rodney paused for a long moment and tears began to well up in his eyes. He said in a soft whisper, "Man, I know God and I know the Bible. But I sure have a tough time following his word."

I looked at him and said, "Well then, that makes two of us. It is hard to follow his plan, isn't it? Sometimes it seems like our plan is better, but I know that in my own life, whenever I try it my way, it always ends up worse than if I did it God's way."

I looked into Rodney's eyes. Tears were now streaming down his face. Whatever I just said hit him straight in the heart. He said, "Man, ain't that the truth."

Without hesitation, I asked, "Rodney, how much do you need for the bus?"

He said the fare was $22.50. I looked into my wallet, and I had exactly $22.00 left. Then I reached into my suit pocket, and pulled out the only two coins I had. Two quarters. Salty tears began burning my cheeks. I looked at Rodney and I said, "I don't know what you're going to use this money for, Rodney. I trust you that it's to go see your mother. But all I know is that this is between you and God."

Rodney looked at me and said softly, "I was telling you the truth, man. I am heading for the bus station right now. God bless you and thank you for your heart."

I watched Rodney run down the street, presumably towards the bus station. After a hundred yards, he turned and yelled "God bless you man!"

I can't be certain where he was headed that hot afternoon.

But I *am* certain that God himself arranged the meeting between us. Rodney's heavenly father had overwhelmed me with his peace and prompted me to say the things this prodigal son needed to hear.

I like to think that Rodney's life turned around that day, but only God knows. Maybe I was Rodney's last chance. Or maybe I was just a stepping stone to his salvation, one of many who would sow good seed into his life. Either way it was a divine moment.

As I walked the remaining blocks to my hotel, the disappointing business presentation was all but wiped from my memory. I thought, *God, surely meeting Rodney is what you had in mind when I asked you to enlarge my territory.*

Packing my suitcase, it occurred to me that God had put me in a business that required thoughtful presentation and clear communication. Success in my field would mean opportunities to touch people's lives in many different ways. And while my prayers in Buffalo were self-centered, God arranged an other-centered encounter beyond my imagination.

I was beginning to see that God wanted me to touch others for him. This I could do, regardless of whether I won or lost in business. Whether I was in a dangerous slum or a posh boardroom. And I saw that he would protect me in either environment. My deodorant definitely failed me that day, but I had a new kind of confidence that came from above: *"For I know the plans I have for you... plans to prosper you and not to harm you, plans to give you hope and a future"* (Jeremiah 29:11).

At the Buffalo airport, I tried to call the consultant to apologize for the lousy presentation I had made. She didn't answer so I left her a voice mail. I told her I thought it was one of the worst train wrecks of my career, and that I was completely thrown off by the three men disrupting the meeting. I figured that even though we didn't win the business, I could at least keep the door open for future opportunities to present to her clients.

When my flight arrived in Detroit, I turned on my cell phone. I had a message. Retrieving my voice mail, I nearly dropped the phone. The consultant had called back to say, "You better perfect that imperfect presentation because you won the business!"

I was shocked.

Surely, God had *"blessed me indeed."*

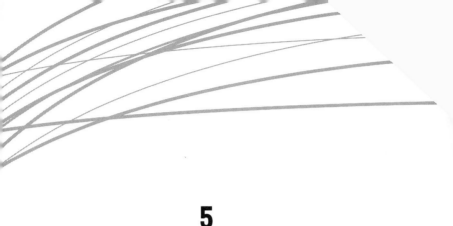

5

HABITS:
Ears Wide Shut

Some people can sleep through an alarm clock. Others can snooze through a noisy thunderstorm. But can you imagine sleeping through an air raid?

On September 7, 1940, Nazi Germany launched a massive air assault on the city of London. From dusk till dawn, 348 long-range bombers pounded the city. For 57 consecutive days, Hitler's *Luftwaffe* dropped tons of bombs on the densely populated area. Off and on for the next two years, squadrons of *Messerschmitts* rained terrible destruction down on the city, killing 30,000 civilians. Known as the Blitz, these nightly air raids were designed to terrorize the populace and force the British government to surrender. But instead of weakening the victim's morale, the bombings actually galvanized the Brits and strengthened their resolve.

Each night, thousands of Londoners would head deep underground to find safety in the city's subway tunnels. As air raid sirens wailed and explosions rocked the surface, families in the "tube stations" waited nervously for daylight. At first

e frightened. But as weeks turned into months, the
the bomb shelters changed. Fear of the unknown was
by a comforting normalcy. Despite the danger and
uncertainty, people began to relax and socialize. Despite the
raging inferno above, they slept soundly in their impromptu
bunkers. The raids which had at first seemed so strange and
disruptive soon became a familiar routine – a *habit*.

And habits can be very powerful things.

A Spanish proverb says, "Habits are at first cobwebs,
then cables." For good or bad, any repeated behavior exerts
a stronger and stronger effect on our thoughts and actions.
English poet John Dryden said, "We first make our habit,
then our habits make us."

Need proof? Many Londoners who lived through the
Blitz *did* suffer from insomnia – but not because of the noise,
because of the *silence* when the bombing finally stopped!

A wiser man than me once said that habits form the basis
of our behaviors, behaviors form the basis of our character,
and our character is who we truly become. The longer we
reinforce our habits and behaviors, the more difficult they are
to change.

The same is true with spiritual routines.

If we repeatedly reject God throughout our lives, it
becomes more difficult to respond and turn to him for answers.
If we get in the habit of ignoring God, it gets increasingly
easier to drown out his voice and dismiss his leadings. Even
when life knocks us over the head with a two-by-four.

A crisis like a death in the family or loss of a job can drop us
to our knees in prayer. Divorce or illness can send us searching
for a higher power. But too often, once the emotional impact
has worn off, the spiritual earplugs go back in. After the attack
on the World Trade Center in 2001, churches in America were
filled beyond capacity with visitors seeking answers in the midst

of the turmoil. But within a few months, attendance fell back to pre-9/11 levels.

Some people have made up their minds to ignore God once and for all. Case closed. Game over. But most people who are ignoring God "today" intend to seek him "later" at a more convenient time of their choosing. They're not completely rejecting God, they're just asking him to please have a seat in the waiting room. The danger here is that the once-tender human heart can get calloused. Resist God's voice often enough and you may become impervious to it until it's too late: *"When I called, they did not listen, so when they called, I would not listen"* (Zechariah 7:13).

In other words, unless you can accurately predict the day you're going to assume room temperature, procrastinating with God could be harmful to your eternal health. No wonder scripture warns us *"Today, if you hear his voice, do not harden your hearts"* (Hebrews 4:7).

Only the transforming power of God's Holy Spirit can break the all-too-common pattern of sensing God trying to reach us, ignoring his offer, and then going on with our life as if he didn't exist...

o   o   o

When Pat was a child, she was exposed to what I call "toxic Christianity" in a home full of religious contradictions. Her mother claimed to be Christian, but instead of experiencing the joy of Jesus, she lived in a gloomy cloud of darkness, fear, and suspicion. Instead of embracing others and sharing her faith, she was worried that the world and its "evil influences" would infect her family. Her children, bearing the verbal brunt of her unhappiness, simply avoided her and her religion.

Her odd mix of legalism and censorship was an awful

distortion of the freedom Jesus promises. Christianity is supposed to be about relationships, but for Pat's mother it was all about rules. Instead of trusting the God of love, she feared the God of punishment. And fear is highly contagious. This poor woman was afraid of going to hell for even the tiniest mistake, and she passed this negativity on to her children.

The pastor at Pat's church reinforced this fear. His message, as Pat calls it, was all "fire and brimstone." Pat never heard the good news that Jesus promises forgiveness and abundant life. Instead, she heard "If you screw up, you will burn in hell!" So at a young age, Pat made a decision: If being a Christian meant being miserable and fearful, she wanted nothing to do with it. As Billy Joel sang in *Only the Good Die Young*, Pat would rather "laugh with the sinners than die with the saints."

Given her grim picture of religion, who could blame her?

Early in my career, I hired Pat to work with me in the investment management business and we became good friends. She had a great sense of humor, and she knew how to keep me humble. At least she tried to. By the time I started my new business, Pat had already retired to spend time with her husband Mel. And when she came out of retirement to work for a competitor, I thought she was out of my life forever. But shortly after we opened our doors, Pat contacted me and we hired her right away. We knew she could be a great addition to our team.

Unfortunately, she wasn't the same Pat I had remembered. Her quick smile and upbeat demeanor were nearly gone. One morning in the office, I felt God place Pat on my heart. For no apparent reason, I had a deep and immediate concern for her well being, the unmistakable impression that she needed help. Later that day, I called her into my office and asked if she was all right. She said "no" and then told me her story.

Pat's husband had suffered a series of minor strokes a few years back. Although the initial impact was insignificant, the doctors suspected that, combined with his other health problems, Mel's mental state would only get worse. Sure enough, Pat noticed her husband was losing his memory. Soon he could no longer remember simple things. Eventually, his condition deteriorated until he totally forgot their life together. For Mel, their wedding and honeymoon never happened. Vacations, anniversaries, birthdays – all gone. As Pat recalled, "It was as if I wasn't even married." There was no love or romance anymore, and their lifetime of shared experiences was erased. With no common bond, she was just another stranger taking care of Mel. The excruciating emotional stress and grinding physical burden were taking a toll.

As she told me her sad story, I felt prompted to tell her about what was going on in my life. I told her how I had kept God out of my life for too long. I shared how after I asked him into my life, incredible changes began to take place within my family. I told her how I came to believe that Jesus was real and that his Holy Spirit was still active in the lives of his people.

Then I asked her where God fit into her life.

She described her childhood growing up around negative Christians. It hurt me to hear the emotional pain and damage misguided religious people had caused in her life. She told me she did believe in some kind of God, but didn't really believe that Jesus was his son, or that he was the only way to heaven. One thing was certain – Pat was convinced the so-called Christians she grew up with were nowhere near paradise.

She also told me about the night an angel showed up in her bedroom to comfort and protect her. She said it was a very real experience, and this supernatural visitation confirmed the existence of a higher power for her. I was amazed to hear what Pat described as "her own personal miracle." I was even more amazed that it didn't spur her into seeking God. To her, it was just an interesting story to tell. To me, an angel sitting on my bed would be more than enough evidence that God is worth pursuing.

That first spiritual conversation started a series of question and answer sessions between Pat and me. The discussions were always lively and I sensed she was beginning to see evidence of God in her own life. Her questions were so penetrating that I often felt inadequate to answer them. So I bought her message tapes on the existence of God and the historical evidence for Jesus. She listened carefully and said she actually enjoyed the compelling arguments. Finally, it seemed like she was searching for answers in the right place.

Whoever said hindsight was perfect sure got it right. I originally thought my "Pat assignment" from God was to simply open the door a crack for the Gospel. But what happened next revealed another reason I was involved in her life. Looking back, I saw once again how God was working behind the scenes long before it became obvious.

Several months after we began our Q&A sessions, Pat came into my office, clearly shaken. When I asked her what was going on, she told me her husband had just been diagnosed with pancreatic cancer. The words hung in the air. Considering his other health problems, we both knew the likelihood of a positive outcome was remote.

As she spoke, a rush of conflicting feelings poured out. She felt sorrow, helplessness, and even guilt for thinking of her husband as a burden. I surprised her by saying I could see God's hand in the whole situation. Just a few months earlier, we had hired a good friend of Pat's named Wanita. Like Pat, this woman had also come out of retirement, and amazingly, Wanita's husband was also stricken with pancreatic cancer. There was no doubt in my mind that hiring this compassionate widow was not a coincidence, but a clear sign God was putting people in Pat's life who could understand and comfort her.

Sadly, just four days after the doctors discovered cancer, Pat's husband passed away. She called me at our northern Michigan cottage to tell me the news. Then she asked me a serious question. Since neither she nor her husband attended a church, she didn't know anyone who could officiate the service and wondered if I would do it. I was shocked and humbled. She said since I was the only person she trusted enough to talk about God with, she figured I could handle the funeral.

My first response was a brave and compassionate "no way." But then a Bible verse popped into my head: *"God never gives you more than you can handle."* I knew my paraphrase wasn't precise, but I figured it was close enough (1 Corinthians 10:13, sort of).

I thought, *OK. God never gives you more than you can handle. Maybe I am supposed to do this for Pat. Maybe God wants me to grow by doing this.* I reflected on this for all of four seconds until I remembered the second half of that verse, *"And he always gives you a way of escape."*

Escape. What a beautiful word. *That is exactly what I need in this situation. I need serious help!* Immediately, I thought of my pal Craig.

Craig was one of our teaching pastors at Kensington Church and occasionally attended our men's group. While he had never met Pat, he knew me well enough to know this was important to me and agreed to do the service. No doubt it was awkward for him because he wasn't sure where the family stood in their faith. Despite that, he did an amazing job explaining God's mercy and love to the captive audience.

At one point, I had the chance to stand up and say a few words. I reflected on how God had prompted me to start the dialogue with Pat so many months earlier. It was the first time most of my employees heard me speak openly about God. The whole experience comforted Pat and she was deeply thankful to Craig and me for the meaningful service.

Being confronted with the brevity of life is the number one wake-up call for most people. So I honestly thought the tragedy of Mel's death would focus Pat's interest on God and the afterlife. I was convinced she would soon realize how much she needed the love of Jesus. While she had expressed feeling God's peace throughout the ordeal, her concept of God was more of an unknowable, impersonal force than the *"friend who sticks closer than a brother"* that we see in Jesus (Proverbs 18:24). In the months following the funeral, she lost interest in our spiritual discussions and stopped asking me questions about God. For Pat, the search for truth was called off and put on hold indefinitely.

I was puzzled.

Since then I've learned that God never stops trying to get our attention: *"Suppose one of you has a hundred sheep and loses one of them. Does he not leave the ninety-nine and go after the lost sheep until he finds it?"* (Luke 15:4).

God wants Pat (and every one of us) to cross the line of faith and become a believer more than anything in the universe. But the action step of turning to him is our own individual responsibility: *"You will seek me and find me when you seek me with all your heart. I will be found by you"* (Jeremiah 29:13-14).

God will pull out all stops to attract our attention, but because of the rules he set up before creation, he won't mess with our free will. He didn't slap the apple out of Adam's hand and he won't force Pat into his kingdom. It's our decision. Our choice to seek him or ignore him. But we must remember – what we do often enough will eventually become a habit. Hopefully, the habit of rejecting him won't become so ingrained into our being that it becomes the core of who we are.

Someone once said, "Bad habits are like a comfortable bed – easy to get into, but hard to get out of." And I believe ignoring God is the worst habit of all.

Pat's story is still being written. By faith, I pray that she will *"seek and therefore find"* the one true God who can save her life forever. My part has been to plant some seeds in Pat's life. I pray that others will water those seeds. And I pray most of all that I will someday get to witness those seeds blossom into a full harvest.

Years later, I led a group study of Rick Warren's *The Purpose Driven Life* in my office. Attendance was voluntary of course, and I wasn't sure who would show up. First day, Pat was there, full of great questions. She's still skeptical, but still seeking. And that is the best habit of all.

○   ○   ○

"So I say to you: Ask and it will be given to you; seek and you will find; knock and the door will be opened to you." (Luke 11:9)

6

TRANSITIONS:
Journey To Manhood

A Jewish boy becomes a man at the ripe old age of 13. If local laws permit and his parents agree, he can be married in a synagogue. But not until he officially becomes a man in a rite of passage as old as the Bible. After completing a year of Hebrew studies taught by his rabbi, the boy is invited for the first time to read from the *Torah* (the first five books of the Old Testament) in the temple.

The boys not only have to read a lengthy passage in Hebrew, they must sing it. And to make it even tougher, there are no vowels printed in the holy writings. So they have to memorize how each word is pronounced. Since touching the actual scrolls is forbidden, a pointer is held just above the page to help the nervous teen make his Semitic singing debut. The service is followed by the *kiddush*, a ceremonial blessing marked by drinking wine and eating unleavened bread. Then it's party time. The *bar mitzvah* is a huge celebration attended by family and friends to mark the transition to manhood.

For the nomadic tribes of East Africa, the difference

between survival and starvation depends on training boys to be strong, courageous men. The key rite of passage for a Massai male is the transition from boy to *moran* or "warrior." The warrior's job is to protect his village from poachers, graze the cattle, and even raid nearby villages for livestock.

The ritual begins with the mass circumcision of boys 13 to 16 by the elders. Next they are sent out into the wilderness for two years to prove their strength and virility. They are allowed no contact with adults and have to survive entirely off the land.

In Australia, aborigine boys drink human blood to become men. In Thailand, Buddhist boys take monastic vows to signal manhood. But what about the average pubescent boy in modern America?

○   ○   ○

A year after we began attending Kensington, I picked up a book for parents of teenage boys called *Raising a Modern Day Knight* by Robert Lewis. Back in the days of knights in shining armor, there was a code of conduct that young men were expected to learn and obey. Values of honor, courage, and chivalry were placed above self-gratification. There was also a series of specific steps to follow if they were to join the brotherhood of knights.

The first step in this pathway was becoming a page – a young servant in the castle who ran errands for the knights. In their teen years, pages could graduate to the rank of squire – a full-time apprentice to a knight. Finally, if a squire passed all of his tests and abided by the code, he could be knighted in a formal ceremony.

From adolescent to adult, each stage of a future knight's life was accompanied by a public ceremony, celebrating each critical step of passage. For a young lad in medieval times, the path to manhood was clearly marked.

Unfortunately in modern culture, boys have little or no idea what it takes to become a man. The route is especially puzzling if there is no father in the household or if he is absent much of the time.

Although I had tried to be an active and involved father, Lewis' book convicted me to become far more intentional in raising my boy to manhood. In fact, I felt prompted to conduct an actual rite of passage ceremony for my son Chad, who was just turning 13. It seemed like an excellent way to remind him that God desired to be in the center of his life and had already laid out a path for him to follow.

Immediately after finishing the book, I thought about involving the group of old friends I took bird hunting every year in my plan. This motley crew was affectionately dubbed the "Skyshooters" by my great-uncle Will. It was back in our college days when we first trekked up to my great-grandparent's cabin on the Au Sable River in northern Michigan for what would become our annual October hunt.

The ritual was the same each year: a big Saturday breakfast followed by the morning hunt, lunch, football on the radio, afternoon hunt, and then a huge dinner of steak and spuds.

Each time we returned from a hunt, my uncle Will would stand out on his porch and yell to us "How many?" We would have to confess that we either got nothing or one measly woodcock. Of course, he would always have at least two fat grouse hanging from his porch which he bagged during his morning stroll to get the newspaper.

Hearing our lack of success, he would reply, "What'ya mean nothing? It sounded like World War II down there." None of us could argue with his metaphor since he had actually fought in the Allied invasion of North Africa in 1943. So we offered up our best excuses: "We never had any good shots" or "The birds always flew up into the sun." To which he would respond, "Aw, you're just a bunch of skyshooters." Luckily for the birds, he was right and our annual reunion became known as the Skyshooter's Weekend.

As I thought about this special gang of buddies who couldn't shoot straight, it occurred to me that each of them also had boys who were 12 or 13. We had always talked about taking our sons with us when they were old enough to hunt, and in Michigan, 12 was the legal age. On top of that, the beauty and ruggedness of the North Country was the perfect setting to conduct what we would later call the "Journey to Manhood."

As I made plans in my head, a chilling thought froze me in my tracks – I had no idea where any of my friends stood in their faith. It made me nervous as I thought about communicating my plan to them. Then it occurred to me that it wasn't *my* plan. It was God's. While praying, he prompted me to write each Skyshooter a letter and enclose a copy of *Raising a Modern Day Knight*. I sent the letters and books in April and I waited to hear back from the group. An entire month went by with no reply. Then two months passed and I still had not heard a thing from anyone. I was pretty discouraged at the lack of response. I worried, *They must think this is a really stupid idea*. But I felt convicted to press on so I picked up the phone.

The first guy I called was Charley. I wasn't really sure what he believed, but I remembered him being an agnostic in college. My fingers trembled as I dialed his number. Charley wasn't home, but his wife Patty answered. I asked her if Charley had received the letter. She told me he had and that they were both blown away by the plan. When she read my letter she had actually cried. She explained how God was not only working in their lives, but at that very moment, Charley was at church, taking classes to become a member!

Encouraged, I called my next friend on the list, Chuck. He told me the whole idea was "count-me-in" amazing and then shared how God was working in his life. Incredibly, Chuck was right in step with me – still seeking and learning but locked into the reality of Jesus. Now even more inspired, I picked up the phone and called the last guy on the list, Greg.

Could I hope for a trifecta?

I knew Greg had grown up Catholic and although he attended church in college, he didn't exactly behave like an altar boy, shall we say. I suspected he was just going through the motions of religion without any real inward change. But when I got him on the phone, his story captivated me. Because of a near tragedy involving his wife, both of them had surrendered to the Lord and had been experiencing his blessings for many years. I was stunned. In all the years Greg and I hunted together, the subject of God never came up. Or maybe I just wasn't listening. Based on the selfish way I lived my life, I'm guessing I was probably just too self-absorbed to notice what was happening around me. In any case, Greg was walking the walk, serving on mission trips, and living a life devoted to Jesus.

I hung up the phone that evening in awe.

Unknown to me, God had paved my way years in advance. Like many times since, I realized right there in my Barcalounger that he had already been at work long before I decided to arrange the ceremony.

The late October weekend arrived quickly, and with a brief detour to the Beef Jerky Factory Outlet (I'm not making this up), Chad and I were headed up north. The ritual was to be held that Friday evening, and the boys knew nothing about it. I remember feeling extremely anxious, praying for nice weather, and hoping that everything would come off well.

Driving past miles of unspoiled aspen, birch, and maple trees, I thought to myself, *When I get up there, I'm going to make sure everything is ready. Then I'm going to climb up and sit on the highest bank of the river. All by myself, I'm going to look out over that valley and personally invite God into the evening.* I was totally resolved that if I did nothing else, I would spend time praying and seeking his guidance.

When we arrived we sucked in lungfuls of crisp fall air and unloaded our bags. I grabbed the guys and we slipped out of camp to arrange the ritual. First, we went down to the river and set up the bonfire. Next, I showed each man where he would be stationed as the boys came down. Distracted by dozens of details, I hardly noticed when darkness fell. Glancing at my watch I saw it was 7:30 p.m. and time for the ceremony to begin.

I gave each boy a flashlight and a slip of paper with a specific time written on it. They were to leave the cabin – alone and unarmed – at the exact moment indicated on their sheet. One by one, they were to walk by Uncle Will's place, down the steps to the two-track road, and over the wooden bridge where they would find us waiting for them. The boys were visibly worried, nervous we were going to play a practical joke on them.

As we walked out of the cabin to get into our places for the start of the evening, I gasped. I had completely forgotten to pray. It was the one thing I wanted to do more than anything else, and I let the distractions of setting up keep me from doing it. First I was sad. Then I was mad. I was so angry at myself that I became totally disengaged from the rest of the group.

As we walked, I was thinking that I would get each of the guys in their places and say some quickie prayer to invite

God into the evening. It upset me that God was only going to get my leftovers.

But God showed me he needs no invitation. Wherever a group of believers gets together to honor him, he shows up big-time: *"For where two or three come together in my name, there I am with them"* (Matthew 18:20).

As I was busy kicking myself, Chuck suddenly stopped us. "Hey guys. Let's gather together right here and say a little prayer for our ceremony." I was amazed. God knew what I needed and he made it happen. I can't remember the exact words Chuck prayed that evening, but it spoke directly to me. At that moment, the peace of God enveloped me and I knew it was going to be an awesome night.

One by one, the boys began their dark, lonely hike down to the ceremony. As they passed Uncle Will's cabin, they headed for the stairs at the top of the hill. Standing next to a tall oak was Chuck, ready to greet them. As each boy approached, Chuck asked him a direct question, "Are you ready to become a young man?"

When a boy answered "Yes!", Chuck responded by quoting King Solomon: *"My son, if you accept my words and store up my commands within you, turning your ear to wisdom and applying your heart to understanding, and if you call out for insight and cry aloud for understanding… then you will understand the fear of the Lord, and find the knowledge of God"* (Proverbs 2:1-3, 5).

Later that evening, Chuck described the combination of bewilderment and relief on the boy's faces.

After the scripture, each boy moved on. At the bottom of the steep stairs they encountered Charley. By the dim glow of a penlight, Charley recited the stirring words of Teddy Roosevelt: "It is not the critic who counts, nor the man who points how the strong man stumbled or where the doer of deeds could have done them better. The credit belongs to the man who is actually in the arena; whose face is marred by dust and sweat and blood; who strives valiantly and spends himself in a worthy cause; who, at best, knows the triumph of high achievement; and at worst, fails while daring greatly, so that his place shall never be with those cold and timid souls who know neither victory nor defeat."

As they continued along the deserted seasonal road toward the bridge, I waited in silence. Standing next to a towering pine, I held a Coleman lantern in one hand and a shaving mirror in the other. I asked each new arrival to look in the glass and answer two questions: "Do you see a young man who is trustworthy and honest, one that others can count on to do the right thing? Do you see a man who, through his actions, will bring honor to God and his family?"

Again we hoped the answer would be "Yes," but I think my son offered the only truthful answer. He said, "Most of the time." As a flawed father and former teenage rebel, I totally appreciated that response.

My son Chad was the third boy to go through the journey, and as he approached me, he said in a soft whisper, "Dad! This is really cool!" Till then I had no idea how the boys were taking all of this, but once Chad came through, I knew it was having the right effect. Looking up into the starry northern sky, I thanked God.

Once they passed by me, they were sent on a journey to the bridge where Greg was waiting for them. He read the passage, *"When I was a child, I talked like a child, I thought like a child, I reasoned like a child. When I became a man, I put childish ways behind me"* (1 Corinthians 13:11).

Then he challenged them, "As you cross over the bridge, you will leave your childhood behind and your journey to manhood will have begun."

As the boys crossed over the bridge, they could see a

blazing bonfire ahead of them. From a distance, they saw silhouettes of unknown men around the campfire. This made them apprehensive. As they drew nearer to the fire, they were thrilled to recognize the men as their grandfathers. None of them knew their grandpas would be with us on this weekend, and there were warm embraces and tears of surprise.

As the last boy went through, each of the dads joined us at the campfire. Gathered around the blaze, I told the young men that since they were now old enough to hunt, they had passed into a new stage. As teenagers they would be faced with many choices, and how they responded would shape the kind of man they would become. I shared that this three-generation ceremony was designed to pass on the values that we as fathers and grandfathers held sacred.

To communicate what it means to be a *real* man, we utilized an acronym. We explained that R stood for "respectful"– of parents, elders, friends, and especially girls. The E stood for "engaged" – with God as the ultimate source of wisdom, and with the world to make it a better place. The A stood for "always honest" – integrity was critical. Finally, the L stood for "leadership" – not always easy because it meant doing the right thing and not going along with the crowd.

As the fire burned down to glowing coals, we came to the final phase of the ceremony. Each of the grandfathers and fathers had written a letter for their young man. Family by family, we read the letters aloud. From the opening lines of the first letter to the final goodbye of the last, there was not a dry eye in the group. Each letter was full of wisdom and love. But what amazed me most was that every page made a strong reference to God. When I began this process, I didn't even know what the fathers believed, let alone the grandfathers!

I finished in prayer and the ceremony came to a close. It had an impact on all of us that I never dreamed possible.

God had shown up in a major way. The boys had the time of their lives and the Skyshooters even had some success with the birds. In fact, the weekend had so many "God moments" I thought it was impossible for him to show up any bigger.

I was wrong.

On Sunday afternoon, as we were cleaning up and getting ready to leave, our young knights asked if they could go into the woods to shoot their paintball guns one last time. We said it was no problem as long as they had packed up their gear and cleaned their rooms. The only caveat was they had to be back in 30 minutes so we could all head home. Agreeing to come back on time, they took off with their high-tech paintball guns towards the forest.

In less than 20 minutes they returned, running as fast as they could. Expecting tardiness, we were amazed when they voluntarily came back early. We said our goodbyes and everyone headed downstate except Chad and me. I still had some chores to finish in the cabin since we were closing it up for the long Michigan winter. For the first time ever, Chad seemed anxious to leave. Too anxious. He said, "Come on Dad. Let's get going."

"But Chad," I said, "There's no need to hurry. We're heading downstate for the Chinook salmon run. We've got all day."

Chad looked a little dejected and said, "Yeah, but Dad, I'd love to get going down there now. Is there anything I can do to help?"

I told him he could pack up the truck with our gear, and he bolted off like a man on a mission to get it done. I thought to myself, *Wow. This weekend really had an effect on him. I've never seen him so motivated.* I soon learned the source of his sudden inspiration.

Chad finished packing the truck and immediately hopped

in the front passenger seat, waiting for me to finish up. As I was locking the front door, I saw something blue out of the corner of my eye. It was a Ford pickup barreling down our long two-track driveway. The pickup pulled around in front of my truck and a huge guy with a scruffy beard and a beat-up hat got out. "Can I help you with anything?" I asked.

He looked all around and growled, "Do you have any young boys here?"

"Well, we did," I replied, "however they all just left. But my son's still here. That's him sitting in the truck." I glanced over to Chad in the passenger seat and all I could see were two beady eyes peering over the dashboard as he slouched down in his seat. "Why do you ask?"

"Well, they shot up my truck with their paintball guns," the man said. I looked into my truck, and with my index finger motioned for Chad to come out. As he slunk toward us, I asked, "Chad, did you shoot this man's truck?" As if he needed to see the evidence, Chad walked to the back of the pickup truck to make a positive identification of three red splotch marks.

He said, "Yeah, that was us."

I told Chad to go inside and get a bucket of soapy water and a rag. While he was scrubbing, Chad apologized a dozen times. When he was done, Chad apologized one last time, slipped back into our truck, and slid down in his seat. I thanked the stranger for holding my son accountable. Nodding, he hopped back in his Ford and drove off. As his truck became a tiny speck I walked back onto the porch. Alone in the stillness and peace of the north woods, I was angry.

I could not believe what had just happened, especially right after our weekend ceremony. I guess at some crazy level I expected everything to be perfect – as if my son would never make another mistake. Of course at his age I made more than my share of screw-ups, but I just couldn't believe he would pull such a dumb stunt after all the talk about being a real man and a leader.

Normally, my reaction to the situation would have been to verbally berate him, question his intelligence, and generally make him feel stupid. Not exactly the type of reaction Jesus would have.

Maybe I could do better if I asked for help. As I put the key in the cabin door, I looked up to heaven and prayed, *Lord, I don't know how to handle this. But you do. What do you want me to do?*

For the first time in my life, I received an instant message back. It was a thought that had to be from God, because there was no way I would ever come up with this idea on my own. His inspiration came streaming into my consciousness and I heard the whisper, *Say nothing.*

I couldn't believe it. I should have been flabbergasted by the fact that God had actually responded to me, but instead I was ticked off. I wanted to argue with him, *What do you mean, "Say nothing?" Is that the best you've got?*

But even at that ungrateful moment, I realized I had actually heard the still small voice of God, and I was determined to follow his advice.

I locked the door, jumped into our Chevy Tahoe, and without saying a word drove out to the front gate. I got out of the truck, closed and locked the gate, and jumped back in. Still not speaking, I pulled out onto the main road and drove for five minutes or so. The silence was, as they say, deafening. As the miles rolled by, I noticed Chad's shoulders shaking. Realizing he was crying, I asked, "What's the matter Chad?"

He looked at me with tears streaming down his face and said, "Dad, that was the dumbest thing I have ever done in my life, and I knew that God was not going to let me get away with it."

I couldn't believe it. Chad was actually acknowledging that God had a plan for his life and that he understood God would do whatever he could to keep him on that path. As I continued to listen silently, Chad took full responsibility for his actions and total accountability for the group. Somehow, he had learned a far greater lesson than I could have ever taught him. All I did was skip the lecture, get out of the way, and let God do his work.

As we drove south to go fishing, our mood brightened, our spirits lifted, and our lively conversation reflected my pride in Chad's breakthrough. I knew that my son had made a big step towards becoming a real man.

God revealed himself that weekend. I came away with an enriched relationship with my son, and I learned something new about Jesus: When he is living in your heart, he doesn't need a special invitation to show up. If you are following his lead he is already with you round the clock. After all, the Journey to Manhood ceremony only happened because I dared to follow his prompting in the first place.

I also learned that God will give us the desires of our heart, as long as they match up with his: *"Delight yourself in the Lord and he will give you the desires of your heart"* (Psalm 37:4).

Jesus knew how much I needed him that evening and he spoke through Chuck to make sure we calmed our hearts in prayer. Jesus also knew that I was handed an incredible teaching opportunity with my sharp-shooting son. Would I fall back on my typical gruff response, or would I look to God for direction? Would I follow my desires or God's?

Thankfully, I looked to him, and in the faintest of whispers, he gave me exactly what I needed to hear.

7

EMBERS:
Rekindling The Flame

"Men wanted for hazardous journey. Small wages, bitter cold, long months of complete darkness. Constant danger. Safe return doubtful. Honor and recognition in case of success."

Antarctic explorer Ernest Shackleton (1874-1922) ran this classified ad in London newspapers before one of his many expeditions in search of the South Pole. Despite – or because of – the ad's negative tone, he received an overwhelming response.

I'm not sure if Shackleton's successful ad was truth in advertising or reverse psychology, but the fact is that certain people are wired by God to jump at a challenge. Tell them something can't be done, and they'll set out to prove you wrong. Like Neil Armstrong going 171 million miles to land on the moon in 1969. Like Roger Banister running the first mile under four minutes in 1954. Or like a teenager named David killing an eight-foot bully with a slingshot in 950 B.C.

Long before I decided to study the Bible, I knew the classic story of David. It's hard to grow up in America without at least hearing how he took down Goliath with a rock and a sling.

As I grew in my faith, I began to see that God not only blessed the historical David, but that he also seemed to have special plans for modern "Davids," too. Especially the ones he was bringing into my life...

○   ○   ○

King David would have admired the risk-takers who started Kensington Community Church back in 1990. Bucking tradition, Steve Andrews and Dave Wilson felt called to start a new kind of church especially for the "un-churched"– people who felt God was irrelevant and had dropped out of organized religion.

To find out why so many were turned off by church, Steve and Dave did a grassroots survey. In 1989, they knocked on 1,400 doors in suburban Detroit, asking people why they didn't go to church. Answers included "Too boring," "Too snobby," "Too greedy," and "Too hypocritical." These candid responses shaped Steve and Dave's vision for a new kind of church that was none of the above.

In March 1990, Steve and Dave passionately recruited 1,600 of their closest church-going friends and strongest supporters to join them in starting this new "seeker friendly" church. 17 said yes. 1,583 said no.

By August, a tiny core team of 40 began praying and practicing in the rented cafeteria of East Hills Middle School in Bloomfield Hills. On September 30, 1990, Kensington held its first public service. Thanks to a well-timed mailer and a providential frontpage article in the Detroit Free Press, an amazing 463 people showed up.

Because these modern Davids were willing to stick their necks out, Kensington has blossomed into a high-impact church with three campuses that over 10,000 people call home. Kensington continues to take on Goliaths and has planted over a dozen daughter churches with a goal of launching 40 multiplying churches by the year 2020 to reach 250,000 people.

When my wife and I started attending Kensington regularly, we discovered another David (literally) who was a teaching pastor in charge of the midweek service called New Community. While younger than the two co-founders, Dave Nelson had a passion for Jesus that burned deeper than anyone we'd ever met. And he had a way of lighting that flame in others. God's timing was perfect because by then, my original blaze of glory had begun to sputter out.

It sounds corny, but as a new believer I had been "on fire for God," and as usual, this kind of newbie exuberance made some Christians nervous. The more mature believers in my own men's group warned me that before long my fire would burn down to coals. It was just a natural process, they said, almost as if it were unavoidable. Being the type-A that I was way back then (Hello, my name is Jeff. I'm a recovering control freak), I was determined this would *not* happen to me.

Unfortunately, my pessimistic friends were correct. Within six months, the honeymoon was over. The flame that had burned so brightly was reduced to glowing embers.

Looking back, I realize what doused the flames.

My first reaction to Jesus flying into our lives the night my wife and I surrendered to him had been to try and make logical sense of it in my head. I wanted to be sure my faith in Jesus was reasonable so I went on a caffeine-fueled quest for knowledge. I read more books in one year than I had in the previous ten. Cramming my head with facts helped solidify my faith intellectually.

For a while, this "head" faith sustained me and helped feed the passion that was burning inside. But it wasn't enough and the fire began to ebb. Something was missing. Something

I couldn't find in any of my reference books. Something I couldn't figure out until a New Community service on a cold Wednesday in December.

Over 1,000 people attended that winter night's service. But if you ask me they might as well have stayed home, because Dave's message was intended 100% specifically for me. How many times in your life have you felt like the pastor was talking directly to you? As if God knew exactly what you needed to hear? I knew so little about the Holy Spirit back then that I just figured it meant I was a slow learner.

Regardless of my spiritual IQ, God was using Dave Nelson that night to personally tutor me. Some would say he was rekindling my *"first love"* (Revelation 2:4). I would say it was more like pouring gasoline on a campfire.

Outside it was 15 degrees and falling. Inside, it felt like 95 and rising. I was starting to perspire. Dave was speaking on Ephesians 1, teaching how we had access to the same *"incomparably great power"* that God used to perform miracles, turn fisherman into apostles, and raise Jesus from the dead!

Dave said we could have the abundant life God promises us – but only if the eyes of our heart could be enlightened. It hit me right there like a George Foreman punch: God was more interested in my *heart* than my *head*.

Dave said that since the heart is so important to God, surrendering it is how we truly "die to ourselves." He used Jesus' words from John 12:24, *"I tell you the truth, unless a kernel of wheat falls to the ground and dies, it remains only a single seed. But if it dies, it produces many seeds."*

As God's searchlight seemed to shine directly on me, Dave challenged us with a question: "How do we die to ourselves and yet physically live?"

The answer, he offered, was to surrender our hearts and our will to Jesus. By doing this, the selfish desires of our hearts are replaced by God's will and his love for everyone. Then our heart will be truly enlightened – filled with God's desires. Then we will begin to experience God's awesome power in our lives.

I left the church that evening with a new intensity. No longer willing to just believe in my head, I was burning to follow God with my whole heart. But what would that look like in everyday life? Wanting to take my spiritual walk to a higher level, I pursued all the educational opportunities my church offered. Then I looked up every passage in the Bible that contains the word "heart" (570 in case you're interested).

Not surprisingly, many heart passages have a similar theme of love and loyalty to God. When Jesus quotes Moses, *"Love the Lord your God with all your heart,"* he calls it the *"first and greatest commandment"* (Mathew 22:37, Deuteronomy 6:5).

Hearing a good sermon can be deeply moving. But there is no greater teaching tool than seeing a message lived out in action. Dave had taught us all a powerful lesson that night about surrendering our heart and will to God. Two weeks later, Dave was challenged to "practice what he preaches" when God asked him to leave his comfortable home, supportive friends, and financial security to follow his leading.

Dave felt the divine call to pack up his family and start a church in – of all the unlikely places – Salt Lake City, Utah. There was no denying it was God's voice because the plan sounded so absurd. Utah has the smallest percentage of Christians per capita of all 50 states – just 2 percent. Crazier still, Salt Lake City is world headquarters for The Church of Jesus Christ of Latter Day Saints. Since founding the city in 1847, the Mormons have grown in power and influence. Starting a fledgling church in the shadow of the imposing Temple Square was going to be, ahem, challenging. Only God could have come up with that one.

At the same time God was speaking to a "David" about Utah, he was also speaking to a "giant" – not Goliath, but Detroit Lions' All-Pro defensive end Luther Ellis. At 6'5" and 320 pounds, Luther is a hard man to say no to. So when the NFL star approached Nelson about starting a church in Salt Lake City, Dave was all ears. After eight seasons with the Lions, Ellis pledged to leave his home church at Kensington and partner with Dave's pioneering team on this fourth-down-goal-to-go challenge.

From the core team's first meeting to their farewell commissioning, there was no question this group of pioneers was called, equipped, and empowered by God himself. Gina and I watched in awe as 20 Kensington families quit their jobs, sold their homes, and left everything familiar to join Dave Nelson in the call to move 2,800 miles west.

Such is the magnetism of a leader who truly surrenders his heart to Jesus.

Dubbed "K2," the new church officially opened its doors in September 2004. Over 600 people came to the first service. The standing-room-only crowd was an amazing testament to God and to those who obeyed his call to leave their complacent lives and join him on an adventure to reach the lost. More visitors are coming each week to K2, not because it's trendy or flashy, but because lives are being changed dramatically. Throughout this predominantly Mormon region, the word is out: The God of David is in their midst.

As news about K2 spreads, they've had to add a third Sunday service to handle the increase. Already, Dave and his gutsy team are preparing financially to plant new churches of their own someday. And in a twist that only God could orchestrate, unexpected bridges of communication and cooperation are being built between the Mormon community and this evangelical outpost.

Clearly, God is moving in amazing ways through K2. But I often wonder what would have happened if Dave had ignored or rejected or postponed God's call to "go west, young man." Would he still be used as powerfully in his former position back home at Kensington?

Maybe.

But I believe God wanted this particular David to stop tending sheep and start slaying giants.

Thankfully, when the call came, Dave Nelson was abiding, praying, and – this is important – listening. His obedient response to what he heard is just another reality check that life is not about us, it's about God. And the only way we can experience that reality is if we let him enlighten the eyes of our hearts.

○   ○   ○

"I pray also that the eyes of your heart may be enlightened in order that you may know the hope to which he has called you, the riches of his glorious inheritance in the saints, and his incomparably great power for us who believe." (Ephesians 1:18-19)

8

CONTROL:
Flipping The Switch

Two things you probably didn't know:

One. My big brother taught me how to whistle. Other skills, too. Like how to build a campfire, ride a minibike, shoot a bird, soap a window, throw a punch, pop a zit, and squeal the tires. Three years older than me, Mike introduced me to *Playboy*, Budweiser, and Columbian marijuana. With him as my guide, I discovered girls, grass, and Neil Young long before I discovered algebra, civics, and history.

Two. A 20-gauge shotgun shell fires an ounce-and-a-half of lead shot. According to some scientists, that's about double the weight of a human soul as it leaves the body at the moment of death.[1]

○   ○   ○

The first time I saw him swing a club I knew he had the gift.

From his first games at age six, my son Chad showed potential to be a great golfer. He was what the pros call "a

71

natural." Yet as he grew older, he wasn't matching the progress of others in his age group. He had the physical talent and could hit the ball long and straight. But the mental part of his game was weak. More than any other sport, golf challenges you mentally, and conquering this aspect of the game is often the difference between success and mediocrity.

To toughen his competitive spirit, I entered Chad in some upcoming youth tournaments. At our first orientation, the organizers brought in a sports psychologist to speak to the boys. Impressed, I approached the speaker afterward and asked if he worked with boys individually. He did, but unfortunately, lived too far away for us to visit him. When I asked for a referral in our area, he gave me the name of his friend, Lee Gardner.

I called Lee on a Sunday evening in May. I told him my 14-year-old son was about to begin tournament play and needed help getting a handle on the mental side of his game. Then I went deeper: I told Lee that Chad had slipped into negative thinking patterns that were affecting not only his golf game, but other areas of life.

Lee explained that he was technically not a sports psychologist. Instead, he described himself as a "life coach." I didn't exactly understand what that meant, but he sounded like a great guy with plenty of insights into the mind of an athlete. For some reason, I had the feeling this complete stranger could help Chad. As we chatted, I glanced at the clock and was surprised to see it was nearly 7 p.m. Apologizing, I said I had to break off and get ready for a group of eighth-grade boys who were coming over to our house from church. There was a long pause on the other end of the line.

"What church do you go to?" Lee asked.

I told him Kensington. He chuckled, then said he was one of the original 40 members who had started the church.

Whoa. A "divine coincidence" like this usually meant God was up to something.

Turned out Lee was the perfect match for Chad. My son would never have identified with the typical cerebral psychologist. But Lee talked to him like an ordinary guy who loved sports. Because there was no psycho-babble or guilt trips, Chad looked forward to his appointments. Not because his dad thought it was a good idea, but because he actually enjoyed the conversations. I was even happier when he told me Lee was a strong Christian who often quoted scripture to make his point.

As Chad's negative thinking began to change, we could see slow but steady progress at home and school. It was also having an impact on the golf course and he was starting to shoot some excellent rounds. Better yet, he learned to bounce back from mistakes and not let bad holes (or bad grades) get to him. Soon he was scoring better on the links and on his report cards.

As Chad's relationship with his mentor grew, Lee and I became personal friends. During one of my son's weekly appointments, I picked up a brochure in Lee's waiting room. On the cover was the single word "Lifeplan." Puzzled by the term, I read on to discover that Lifeplan was a process of going back through your life and looking at major "turning events" to uncover how you may have allowed faulty thinking to shape your character. As I held the brochure, my mind slipped back to the spring of 1987...

○   ○   ○

When I was 24, my older brother Mike committed suicide. He had been diagnosed with depression and was an alcoholic. Seven years of substance abuse counseling and medical treatment failed to help. He drifted from place to place, finally landing in a coldwater flat in Detroit's tough east side. Long before superstar Eminem made *Eight Mile* a well known address, my brother moved in a few blocks from where the rapper grew up. Unemployed, lonely, and strung out on drugs, he finally ran out of reasons to keep on living.

On the Thursday before Good Friday, he decided to end the pain once and for all. As the rest of our family prepared to celebrate Easter break, Mike loaded the old Remington shotgun we used to hunt birds with as boys. With our parents and sister away in Florida, he drove back to the empty home where he had grown up. At about 10 a.m. he sat down in his childhood bedroom for the last time.

By the time I arrived at the scene, my wife Gina was already there, surrounded by police and detectives. I remember crying as I raced over from my office. And I remember crying as I hugged Gina. But the tears stopped immediately when I changed into my "work" mode. Like flipping a switch, I went from Jeff-the-grieving-brother to Jeff-the-man-in-charge. I did not want my parents to come back and see the mess in their house, so I fastidiously cleaned the room where their first-born had died. Then I told them to stay in Florida until the funeral, insisting that I take care of all the arrangements.

The funeral was held the day after Easter, and while I "permitted" myself to mourn at the service, I returned to work the very next day.

○   ○   ○

If you take your life with a shotgun do you hear the blast?

I've asked myself that question since the day my older brother pulled a Kurt Cobain and took a pointblank shortcut into Hamlet's "undiscovered country."

Like the lead singer of *Nirvana*, Mike battled drugs and depression. Battled them for so long he was willing to bet that whatever lies on the other side of suicide could only be an improvement. And like Kurt, he put the shotgun barrel in his mouth so he wouldn't miss. That's pretty much where the similarities between Mike and Kurt end. When my brother's death was discovered, there were no reporters, no fans, and no candlelight vigil.

Just me with a bucket and a rag.

○   ○   ○

I had long suspected that I had never processed my brother's death appropriately. Oh, sure, as a businessman, I took proper care of the legal details. But I skipped over dealing with the emotional trauma and plunged back into my career as quickly as possible. Eager to get back to normalcy, I blocked the tragedy out of my head and stayed busy. Now, 15 years later, I sensed God nudging me that the Lifeplan might bring the healing and closure I needed. I made an appointment with Lee that afternoon.

In our first session, Lee looked at the patterns of my life – including some that may have been reinforced by my brother's violent death. He validated that I was (big surprise) a control freak. Whenever things got too frenzied in my life, I retreated to a place I felt I could control. Usually that meant my job as an investment manager. During our sessions, Lee asked hundreds of questions. But his queries about my brother were the most revealing.

As Lee probed, memories of that dark holiday started coming back to me – first as a trickle, then as a steady gush of words and images I had pushed down for years…

Squad cars. Ambulance. Neighbors. If I had been there, I

might have stopped him. But I wasn't. Wearing his favorite blue jeans, my brother walked into his upstairs bedroom, cocked the shotgun, and pulled the trigger. *Police. EMS. Coroner.* Ladies and gentlemen, my beloved brother Mike has left the building. Not in a shiny black limousine. In a shiny black bag. A shiny black rubber bag with a huge zipper. *Shock. Questions. Disbelief.* I tried for hours to scrub away any evidence of how he died, scrubbing hard, scrubbing like Lady Macbeth, scrubbing until the blood from my knuckles mingled with his. *Soap. Water. Bleach.* Nothing worked on the carpeting. My wife and I finally ripped it out down to the carpet tacks, rolled it up, and threw it in a dumpster behind a school. If only I could have tossed my guilty conscience in with it.

After hearing my story, Lee asked, "Do you think there was something you could have done differently while your brother was alive?"

I admitted I always regretted being unable to unlock something in my brother to help him see the goodness and joy in life. I told him that I'd always felt partly to blame. That I could have – and should have – done more.

Lee looked at me without blinking, "So you think you could have saved your brother?"

Tearfully I whispered, "Yes."

"So, in other words, you think you're God."

"Ouch," I winced. "That hurts." But I got the point. I was such a compulsive controller that I thought even my brother's life depended on my actions and force of will. I was totally frustrated over being unable to make Mike see things that seemed so blankety-blank (not my exact words) obvious to me.

Lee explained that only God can "fix" people, and even then only if they agree to be fixed. *Wait. Say that again. What just hit the floor? My chin?* Guilt fell off my shoulders like a

50-pound backpack. He said that each person has a free will to make good or bad choices. To obey or rebel. To live in relationship with Jesus or stubbornly go it alone. My job was to offer God's hope and forgiveness to people, but I couldn't force them to believe. Nor could I shield them from the consequences of not believing: *"I have set before you life and death, blessings and curses. Now choose life, so that you and your children may live"* (Deuteronomy 30:19-20).

We worked through other areas in my life where control was an issue – marriage, raising kids, running a business. The Lifeplan was a great eye-opener that helped me surrender more facets of my life to God. But how could I remember these lessons in the stress and crush of my hectic workdays?

The answer was "the tool."

Lee told me to go out and buy a gardening tool to hang in my office to remind me I was simply God's instrument. Poking through flea markets, I found an antique shovel, carved completely out of wood. On the handle, I inscribed, *"My Father is the gardener"* (John 15:1).

Then I added my own prayer: "Lord, let me be the instrument of your will." Today, this shovel of surrender hangs in my office, reminding me that God is the Lord of the harvest and I am only his willing tool: *"So neither he who plants or he who waters is anything, but only God, who makes things grow"* (1 Corinthians 3:7).

Spending time with Lee brought healing to many areas, including the suppressed pain I felt over my brother's death. In the months following the tragedy, I'd heard hurtful whispers about "the unpardonable sin." For years after, I agonized over the question "Does God forgive suicide?" My logical mind even wondered if Mike *could* be forgiven since the opportunity to repent was gone the instant he pulled the trigger.

Then I began to understand that Mike didn't die because

of a desire to usurp God's authority, but because of a disease which overpowered him.

Like millions of others, my brother suffered from a mental condition he didn't ask for that caused unimaginable torment. Why, I wondered, would succumbing to one illness (like depression) be an "unforgivable act" while dying from another (like cancer) was a "brave fight?" If God doesn't punish us for being physically ill, why would he punish us for being mentally ill?

The death certificate listed a gunshot wound as the cause of death, but I knew the real reason was a disease that brought unrelenting mental and emotional pain. In Mike's depressed world of isolation and fear, life became intolerable.

Before medicine diagnosed depression as an illness, the church diagnosed it as a mortal sin, telling grief-stricken families that suicide victims went straight to hell. Until recently, people who took their own lives were buried in unmarked graves in areas of cemeteries reserved for the worst criminals.

But where the church was harsh, God was gracious. Nowhere in the Bible does he restrict his forgiveness to certain "categories" of sin, or limit his grace to a certain "time period." My view is that if a person accepts Jesus Christ as his savior at some point in his life, he is forgiven of all his sins – past and future. Romans 8:1 assures us *"there is now no condemnation for those who are in Christ Jesus..."*

Nobody lives a perfect life, not even the most devout Christian. Writing to believers, the Apostle John said, *"If we claim to be without sin, we deceive ourselves"* (1 John 1:8). We should try our best not to stumble, *"But if anyone does sin, we have one who speaks to the Father in our defense – Jesus Christ"* (1 John 2:1). Any believer can screw up – even after we become passionate Christ followers – but our acts of disobedience do not separate us from the one who promised to never leave us or forsake us (Hebrews 13:5).

I believe that life is a precious gift from God. And of course I believe that suicide was not God's will for my brother. But I also believe that because Mike had given his life to Christ, I will see him again in heaven someday. Meanwhile, I'm certain about where he is and who he is with. My family has drawn amazing strength from this blessed assurance, and each of us has felt Mike's positive presence in our lives. Even his nephew (who never met him) says he has talked to him in his sleep. My parent's faith, which could have been devastated by the experience, has deepened over the years as they await the ultimate family reunion.

Lee also helped me see that God has marching orders for each of us, and that we get into serious trouble when we substitute our plan for his. Which is why I spend time listening to God each morning. A good soldier never heads off to battle without first checking in with his commander to receive orders. Neither do I. And that, to paraphrase Robert Frost, has made all the difference.

Through my "chance" encounter with Lee, God has blessed my entire family. His constructive influence helped me realize (again) that God uses earthly people to fulfill his heavenly will. Obviously, God knew I was dragging around the terrible baggage of my past, and he thrust precisely the right person in my path to help me unload.

Lee has continued working with my son, and also formulated a Lifeplan for my wife. He remains an ongoing source of wisdom and owes me a big cut of his fees for this shameless plug (kidding). Thanks to his counsel, I'm no longer the uptight freak who tries to control everything (okay, except for the weather, the stock market, the flow of traffic, and a few thousand other things). I've learned that God controls my future, and I am forever secure in his love – no matter what troubles or hardships life may bring.

○   ○   ○

"Who shall separate us from the love of Christ? Shall trouble or hardship or persecution? ...I am convinced that neither death nor life, neither angels nor demons, neither the present nor the future, nor any powers, neither height nor depth, nor anything else in all creation, will be able to separate us from the love of God..." (Romans 8:35-39)

---

1 For thousands of years, people have believed the human soul has a definite physical presence. In 1907, Dr. Duncan MacDougall of Haverhill, Massachusetts actually tried to weigh this soul. In his office, he had a special bed built upon delicately balanced platform beam scales to weigh terminally ill patients in their last moments of life. He published studies concluding that we all lose 21 grams at the moment of death. Whether his findings amount to junk science or clinical fact is still contested.

9

ARMOR:
Hammer Time

Jesus could have been a butcher. Or a baker. Perhaps even a candlestick maker (sorry about that). But God chose for him to be a carpenter. Why?

His father, Joseph, was a skilled woodworker. The Greek word describing his trade is *tektron*, and it implies master builder. In Israel, most Jewish boys entered the family business. Especially in small, remote towns like Nazareth. Career hopping was rare, and sons – particularly firstborn sons – inevitably followed their dad's profession.

Their family business or vocation might even become their nickname.

In ancient times, children were named for one of three things: their father, where they were from, or their occupation. For instance, "Smith" is a very common name because blacksmiths, coppersmiths, and silversmiths were once identified by their line of work.

Likewise, Jesus may have been known to neighbors and friends by several names: Jesus the Son of Joseph, Jesus of

Nazareth, or Jesus the Carpenter – especially in his immediate surrounding area. But one moniker that didn't go over big with the locals was his new title of "prophet."

His hometown crowd was puzzled how a neighbor they grew up with could transition from master builder to master teacher: *"...he began to teach in the synagogue, and many who heard him were amazed. 'Where did this man get these things?' they asked"* (Mark 6:2).

His blue-collar occupation and his family tree were no secret to them: *"Isn't this the carpenter? Isn't this Mary's son?"* (Mark 6:3).

No doubt some thought the man who used to fix their broken chairs had gotten uppity. They resented his growing fame and were ticked off by his new role: *"And they took offense at him"* (Mark 6:3).

The Bible doesn't mention the Son of God swinging a hammer, but the majority of wandering rabbis had a trade to support their schooling and teaching. There's no reason to doubt that even the adult Jesus could have pitched in as a carpenter. In the second century, church historian Justin Martyr wrote, "He was in the habit of working as a carpenter when among men, making plows and yokes; by which he taught the symbols of righteousness and an active life."

We may never know what Jesus yelled when he hit his thumb in the workshop. But we can be certain of this: He became adept at his craft. Up until age 30, he probably helped support his family by creating farm tools, beds, and tables. He may have built ox carts, gates, lamp stands, even coffins – the very same items he used as object lessons in his parables.

In the summer of 2002, God brought a very special builder from Windsor, Ontario into my life. And while the carpenter from Canada was working on my *house*, the carpenter from Nazareth was working on his *heart*...

○   ○   ○

When we moved to the country, the house we bought had a charming old outbuilding on the property. The exterior was brick with rough hewn beams and barn wood on the inside. By the look of it, I guessed it may have been a stable back in the 1930s. For the first four years, we used it mainly for extra storage. Then during my prayer time that summer, I felt prompted by God to renovate the building and convert it to a guesthouse.

Gina's grandmother, "Nanny," was nearing 80 and would soon need extra care. Living in her apartment was no longer viable. She complained of loneliness and was becoming absent-minded. But whenever she stayed with us for a weekend, she perked up and her mind seemed sharper. She was not nearly as forgetful and she felt happier. Since Nanny couldn't afford assisted living, we began feeling like the guesthouse project might be a perfect fit for her.

I prayed and asked God to show me his choice for contractor.

The next day I went to church. After the service, I ran into one of the guys from my men's group who worked in our community outreach program. Steve was one of over 500 volunteers in a team called "Reach" who helped inner city people find food and shelter. Since a big chunk of their pro bono work was rehabbing houses, I figured my friend might know a carpenter who needed work. When I asked him, he rocked back on his heels. Shaking his head in disbelief, he said he just talked to a carpenter not five minutes earlier. Seems a Reach volunteer had just walked up out of the blue and asked, "Hey, Steve, if you know anyone in need of a builder, let me know, would you? I could really use the money right now."

Looking around the crowded lobby, Steve said, "I'm

pretty sure he's still around. Wait here and I'll find him." He came back two minutes later, and introduced me to a capable-looking man named Dave.

Another divine "coincidence."

Dave began my job immediately, and it soon became apparent that what God had in mind was far more than just a business arrangement. Dave was going through a knock-down drag-out divorce with two sweet kids caught right in the middle of it all. Between loads of drywall, he described what led to the agonizing breakup. He still loved his wife and wanted things to work out. But he had found out late in his marriage that he suffered from clinical depression. He admitted he was difficult to live with and confessed to making lots of mistakes as a husband and father.

The bright spot in Dave's story was that he had recognized his weaknesses and given his heart to Jesus a few years earlier. But despite knowing that God was real and active in his life, positive change came slowly.

Too slowly for his wife.

The title of Toni Braxton's hit song, *Unbreak My Heart*, hints at the difficulty of repairing broken relationships. Those of us who gave our lives to God later in life know it's hard to heal the pain we've caused others, and harder still to undo years of bad habits, wrong thinking, and selfish behavior. Sadly, it doesn't happen overnight. By the time Dave met Jesus, the damage had been done. Now his wife was filing divorce papers and requesting custody of his 2-year-old daughter and 5-year-old son.

Dave and I soon began meeting for lunch every couple of weeks or so. My passion for Jesus was growing, and I had recently attended a seminar called *24/7 With Jesus*. Taught by my friend, Craig Mayes, it was the fuel I needed to get the flame roaring. Craig's seminar taught me how critically important it was to spend time with God. That week, I literally switched my priorities – in writing – and rearranged my schedule to free up time every morning to read the Bible and pray.

True confession: I am not a morning person. I hate getting up early. But I knew that morning was the quietest part of my day. Because my relationship with Jesus had become the most important affiliation in my life, I was determined to make the hard choices necessary to carve out quality time for him.

Dave the carpenter also needed to make some changes. Like me, he needed someone to hold him accountable for keeping up his spiritual practices. At each lunch meeting we compared notes and I continually challenged him to spend more time with God and less with negative people.

After a dozen high calorie get-togethers, Dave began to trust me enough to really open up. But while I was trying my best to help him, it seemed like everyone else was trying to hurt him. And they were succeeding. His ex-wife and his in-laws went out of their way to put him down. Former friends ostracized him. Suffering from the insults of relatives and the emotional pain of separation, he wondered if Jesus (or anyone else) loved him.

Call it spiritual warfare or spiritual immaturity, but new Christians like Dave are particularly vulnerable to falling back into their old ways and self-destructive patterns. Even though I was more mature than Dave, I tried hard not to get cocky about it. In fact, I sensed God put Dave in my life for two reasons: First, to inspire him to a deeper relationship with Jesus. Second, as a warning to me.

By watching Dave's spiritual tug of war, I saw how vulnerable and weak any of us can become if we don't guard our hearts: *"So if you think you are standing firm, be careful that you don't fall!"* (1 Corinthians 10:12).

I was more than a little sad when Dave finished the

guesthouse a few months later. Fortunately, when the work was over our friendship wasn't. About 90 days later, I felt led by God to hire Dave again. I didn't know why at the time, but I dreamed up a second project that gave us an opportunity to catch up. He started the job on time, but I noticed he was not as reliable as before. One day he called to say something had come up and he wouldn't be able to make it out to the house. When I asked what was going on, he was defensive and dodged my questions. Eventually I dragged the real reason out of him – his depression medication was no longer working. To make matters worse, his ex-wife was playing games with him over their children again and it was tearing him apart.

I told Dave straight up that it was no coincidence our paths had crossed again. It was obvious to me that God was intervening and had brought us back together for a reason. I explained how severe depression had played a huge part in my own family's life. Not only had my daughter struggled with it, but I had suffered from an episode when I experienced a major failure early in my career. I admitted it was only by the grace of God and the love of my wife that I made it through that awful time.

Suddenly, Dave was all ears.

Often, God will use our weaknesses to demonstrate his power and to accomplish his will. I sensed God was using me in this way with Dave. From my own personal experience, I knew some of the anguish he was going through and could relate to him more directly. "Been there, done that" is a powerful help when you're counseling a hurting person.

If God helped me battle depression, it was proof he could also help Dave. He is *"the God of all comfort, who comforts us in all our troubles so that we can comfort those in any trouble with the comfort we ourselves have received from God"* (2 Corinthians 1:3-4).

Once again, the accountability lunches became part of

our routine. I suggested Dave see the same doctor who was so helpful with Kira. He said he would give Dr. Steve a try. He also told me about his recent spiritual insight.

He had been reading Bruce Wilkinson's *Secrets of the Vine*, and especially enjoyed the metaphor of us being connected to God in a living relationship like a branch to a vine. It got him wondering, *What happens if a branch falls into the dirt and grows along the ground?*

From personal experience, we both knew the answer: It cannot bear any fruit. The dirt and mud prevent the sunlight from warming the branch sufficiently to produce grapes. The only way the branch can produce fruit again is if someone picks it up, cleans it off, and props it up where it won't fall again.

Dave saw himself as the trampled branch, lying on the ground, covered in mud – mud slung by a critical father, unforgiving ex-wife, and disapproving in-laws. Somehow, he knew only Jesus could lift him up, wash him off, and put him in a position to bear fruit. Somehow, in the midst of his pain, he knew he needed to find his way back to scripture and prayer.

Like all of us, Dave is still a work in process. But thanks to God's indwelling Spirit, he is no longer a do-it-yourself project. I like to think he will eventually find peace with himself through the love of Jesus, but it's really up to him. One thing is certain – God's power of renewal and rebirth is available to everyone: *"He is patient with you, not wanting anyone to perish, but everyone to come to repentance"* (2 Peter 3:9).

Somebody once said the hardest thing about Christianity is that it's so "daily." Dave needs to keep seeking Jesus and his truth every day. Not once every seven days at church. *Every* day. As soon as we cool down and back away from God, we create space in our hearts for the negative garbage we're bombarded with. As we drift away, our motives become mixed, our mission becomes muddled, and our thoughts become impure.

Living in the dangerous, decadent Roman Empire, the apostle Paul knew how to think positively in a very negative world: *"Whatever is true, whatever is noble, whatever is right, whatever is lovely, whatever is admirable – if anything is excellent or praiseworthy – think about such things"* (Philippians 4:8).

If my carpenter friend – or any of us – neglects Paul's advice and slips into wrong thinking, he'll start to forget who he is and what his purpose is on earth. According to the Westminster Shorter Catechism (written in 1642), the chief end of man is to "glorify God and to enjoy him forever." But Satan would love to distract us from this goal.

In his book *Uprising*, Erwin McManus explains how the devil waits for a small void to appear, a little area in our heart that we reserve for our own selfishness or self-pity. When he sees an opening, the evil one tries to create even more space in our heart for him and his lies.

How do we show Satan a "No Vacancy" sign? By fortifying our faith on a daily basis. Americans spend $2 billion a year on burglar alarms and home security systems. We've got motion-detectors in our houses, the Club on our steering wheels, and anti-virus software on our computers. But God never tells us to guard our plasma TV or our new car or even the family hard drive. Instead, he says to guard our heart. In fact, he says to guard it more carefully than anything else in the world: *"Above all else, guard your heart, for it is the wellspring of life"* (Proverbs 4:23).

Only then can we experience the wellspring – the primordial source of a flowing stream – of life that God has promised us. And only then can we enjoy him forever.

10

RESPONDING:
Cleared For Takeoff

To my right, a red-tailed hawk circled lazily, floating effortlessly on thermal currents rising from the hot sands below. To my left, shimmering ribbons of turquoise water melted into azure, then darkened into a deep blue that stretched to the horizon. Flying low over the treetops, our small plane startled a nest of eaglets perched in a stubborn red oak blackened by lightning a hundred storms ago. The Cessna's single engine echoed through dark forests unchanged since French trappers piled their canoes with beaver pelts here in the 1600s.

Scanning the terrain for landmarks, my 79-year-old pilot had the sharp eyes and steady hands of a man half his age. Pulling back on the stick, he slowed the plane to just shy of stalling, then banked left so I could get a clear view of the dunes below.

Stretching for eight miles along the Lake Michigan coastline, the Sleeping Bear Dunes soar 450 feet above sea level. Formed by prevailing westerly winds blowing across the lake, mountains of shifting sand stretch inland like a glacier, cutting sugar white paths through the old-growth forest of aspen, pine, and birch. Since childhood, I had been one of the 100,000 or so sunburned visitors who climbed the massive dunes each summer. Seeing them from the air was a moving experience I was glad to be sharing with one of the most remarkable men I'd ever met.

A retired surgeon, Ted had started a second career at age 65 as an aerial photographer, flying thousands of hours over remote northern Michigan. Toughened by years as a bomber pilot in WWII, Ted faced life with courage, curiosity, and a pioneering spirit. He never lost his boyhood passion for flying, and I half wondered if somehow he was defying the aging process by defying gravity so often.

○   ○   ○

It was a message by Dave Nelson that rekindled my passion to know Jesus at a deeper level. And it was a seminar called *24/7 With Jesus* that urged me to make space for God in my life. But it was my experience with Ted that pushed me past the point of no return.

By this time I had figured out that if I hung around Jesus long enough he would eventually use me on a project. But working with the God-squad still depended on two things: First, would I put myself in a position to hear from him consistently? Second, when I did hear from him, would I respond?

In the summer of 2002, I got a chance to answer both questions…

It was August, and my family and I were enjoying a long weekend at Elk Lake, near Traverse City, Michigan. On Saturday morning, I woke early enough to see the sun rising over the hills surrounding the lake. Not being a morning person, this is a sight I rarely see. But on this particular morning, I felt like I had been awakened by God for some unknown reason. Careful not to disturb anyone, I quietly tiptoed onto the deck and marveled at the beautiful orange sun just cresting over the trees.

I sensed something tugging at me, inviting me down to the lake. I ducked back inside, grabbed my Bible, and walked down to the dock. I sat on the weathered planks and looked across the water. It was a picture-perfect summer morning. As waves gently lapped against the shore, the only sound was the birds chirping a conversation they'd started hours ago. Soon the sun was high enough to take the chill off the early morning air.

Warmed by the slanting rays, I sat cross-legged on the dock and began reading my Bible. Then I shifted into my prayer time. At this point in my spiritual journey, I prayed in a very precise sequence: first for myself and my family, then for my extended family, then for my friends, and finally for requests made by others. Suddenly, in the middle of my prayer sequence, I was totally interrupted by the still small voice of God. Streaming into my consciousness was a thought that was totally out of order and out of place – yet I heard it distinctly, *Call Ted.*

I remember being so thrown off my routine that I actually looked up toward God and thought, *Can you just hold on? I'm not at the point where I am praying for my friends yet!* As if to say "chill and be still," the words came again, *Call Ted.*

Puzzled, I finished my prayers hastily, and resolved to call Ted later that day at his home in Traverse City.

Walking back toward the cottage, I wondered about the strange request. Ted was a former financial client, and through our business relationship we had become good friends. The fact that he was nearly twice my age made no difference. I felt as close to this WWII vet as I did to any of my college buddies. Ted was one of those bigger-than-life men who was so intriguing that I simply had to get to know him. From our first meeting, I admired this former doctor's unique lifestyle and sense of adventure. After retiring from his practice, he started an aerial photography business so he could fly as much as possible. At 79, Ted was more full of life than most of my contemporaries.

Back in October of 1999, Ted mysteriously fell into a deep depression and was unable to come out of it. He was seeing doctors, but nothing seemed to be working. Finally, in December, his wife asked if I could speak to him. Rather than calling him on the phone, I decided to write him a letter.

Ted and I had always loved to communicate through old-fashioned letter writing. To this day, I have stacks of his treasured letters stored away. In my note, I told him that I too had gone through a period of severe depression. I confided that I never thought it would happen to me, because like him, I was usually upbeat and optimistic. I explained how I had failed to see the warning signs, and after a month of sleeping only two to three hours a night, had fallen hard into fearful and pessimistic thinking.

As Ted read and re-read my letter of empathy and encouragement, he realized he wasn't alone with this disease, and began to become his old self again. In his words, the letter helped him "snap out of it." He wrote me back to say as much, and thanked me profusely for my concern and candid advice. From that point on, we became brothers in this journey of life, and we wrote or called each other often.

Then in 2002, Ted told me he'd been diagnosed with prostate cancer. The doctors were confident they had detected it early enough, and he was scheduled for surgery to have it removed. I never had any doubt he would pull through. Ted was just one of those strong-willed guys who were unusually healthy and active for their age. After all, he still skied Aspen every year with a group of pals, and flew his plane regularly. In fact, he was in such good shape that he flew a writer from *National Geographic* over the Leelanau Peninsula for an article on watershed pollution.

Knowing Ted, I figured this cancer thing was just another bump in the road for him. And I was right. When I called him in March, he said the surgery had gone well, and the doctors felt they had removed all of it. I spoke to Ted again in April, and he said he felt fine and was thrilled because the FAA had just renewed his pilot's license. That is not a privilege extended to many octogenarians!

All seemed well until I received God's unmistakable dockside message.

The day God prompted me to call Ted was three months after I had last spoken with him. Mind racing, I walked back up to the cottage and told my wife about my strange experience. I told her it freaked me out a little bit, and that I was almost afraid to make the call. I also told her that scared or not, I had no choice, because it was God's will. But as the day wore on, I found a hundred excuses to "conveniently delay" my call. In the late afternoon, we even had some friends over for a barbecue. Before I knew it, the sun was setting, and I was running out of time. Apprehensively, I sat on the porch steps and slowly dialed the phone.

Ted's wife, Jean, answered.

"Hi Jean," I said nervously, "It's Jeff. I haven't spoken to you in a while, and I was just calling to see how you and Ted are doing."

There was a pause on the other end of the line. "Well, Jeff, Ted is not doing very well."

My heart sank deep into my chest, and I asked her what was going on.

"Well, the cancer came back, and this time it has invaded

his spine. The doctors say there is really nothing they can do for him, and they only give him a few months to live."

I was devastated.

I could barely put together a cohesive sentence. I told Jean that I was coming back up north the following weekend, and wondered if it would be all right if I stopped by to see Ted. Jean said Ted would love that, so I promised I would see them both the following Saturday.

I hung up, dropped the phone on the porch, and began to cry.

My friend. My hero. The man I thought was invincible was dying. I cried harder that evening than I had in years. Hearing the commotion, my kids came around the porch to see what was wrong. I told them to get their mom, and when Gina came out, the four of us huddled together. Between sobs, I told them Ted was dying. We gathered in for a group hug, praying and grieving for the man each of us had grown to love.

The next day, I drove home alone, leaving Gina and the kids to stay on for the week. I was consumed with thoughts about Ted, remembering our times together. As I drove south on the I-75 freeway, I felt prompted again. This time, the still small voice said, *You should write Ted a letter.*

The idea of a letter should have been obvious to me, since we had written back and forth for years, but it hadn't occurred to me until then. Gripping the steering wheel, I thought to myself, *This is a great idea. I'll write Ted and tell him how much he has meant to my life.*

As I began to think about what to write, nothing crystallized. Because I wanted the wording to be just right, I decided to wait until I had enough quality time to craft truly beautiful prose. I figured I would go up and see Ted next weekend anyway, and I could easily send him the letter some time after our visit.

At least that was my plan.

The following evening, I was on the computer checking e-mails when I was interrupted again. That whisper that seems to come from nowhere said, *You should write that letter now.*

I actually remember looking up again and replying, "Really?"

Yes. You should write that letter right now, was the inaudible reply.

After my experience on the dock, I knew better than to hesitate, so I started writing immediately. Problem was, I still had no idea what I wanted to say. I must have rewritten the opening line 20 times. Getting nowhere, I finally took my hands off the keyboard. I folded my fingers together and prayed, *Lord, I can't write this letter. I don't know what to say to an old man who knows he is dying. But you know, Lord. You know what you want me to say. Will you please write this letter for me?*

When I put my fingers back on the keyboard, they no longer seemed under my control. For the next 30 minutes, I wrote non-stop. Fingers flying, tears streaming down my face, I knew this was one of the most poignant and powerful letters I had ever written. I also knew full well who the real author was.

The next day was Tuesday, and I mailed the letter from work. I figured it went out in the late evening mail and probably left Detroit on Wednesday. I drove back up to Elk Lake on Friday afternoon, and the minute I set foot in the cottage, the phone rang. I picked it up, and was surprised to hear Ted's son, Jack, on the other end. He was calling to say Ted had passed away that morning. He died in his own home, with his family gathered around him.

My heart sank again, but this time it was not from grief, but from regret for not sending the letter sooner. Angry at myself, I told Jack I had already grieved for his father. I told him I had cried long and hard over the weekend, and that I had accepted the inevitability of his father's death.

"However," I sputtered, "what has me really upset right now is that I sent a special letter to your father this week, and I'm afraid it isn't going to arrive until today."

Jack paused, and when he finally spoke his voice sounded almost jubilant. "Jeff, the letter came yesterday. My dad's entire immediate family was there, and I read your letter out loud to him. I have to tell you, that was one of the most beautiful letters I have ever read. And I am certain that my father heard every word of it."

I hung up the phone with Jack, and stumbled out onto the deck, completely in awe of God. I was in awe of the fact that he loved Ted so much that he wanted to get a message to him. And I was in awe that God would use me to be his messenger. But most of all, I was in awe of how perfect God's timing is. If I had hesitated for one moment longer or questioned whose voice I was hearing, I'd have blown the most incredible divine moment I had yet experienced in my short walk with Jesus.

Erwin McManus, author of *Seizing Your Divine Moment*, says God puts divine opportunities in front of us all the time. Unfortunately, as the prison warden in *Cool Hand Luke* tells inmate Paul Newman, "What we have here is a failure to communicate." The failure is one of two things: Either we don't put ourselves in a position to hear from God, or when we do, we fail to respond.

I am certain God wants to use all of us in some way, but the responsibility is ours to *"seek his face always"* (Psalm 105:4). That's the only way we can know him intimately enough to recognize his voice when he speaks into our lives.

Because God is eternal, the story didn't end with Ted's death, and it continues to touch people's lives. Here's an example: Two weeks after his passing, they held a packed-out funeral for Ted. So many people from out of town wanted to attend, they had to delay the service to allow for travel time. As the crowds swelled, the church couldn't accommodate everyone, so they improvised a video overflow room. In his homily, the presiding minister said, "I would love to tell you that I knew Ted really well. But I did not, for he was a private man. Instead, let me read to you parts of a letter from someone who did." Suddenly, over 500 people from around the country heard what God had to say to Ted that day.

I'm convinced that this is exactly how God speaks to us – through promptings, convictions, gentle whispers, and streaming thoughts. As I look over my spiritual life so far, I realize the times when I've felt God's presence most clearly were the times when my morning scripture reading and prayer time were the most consistent.

In my marriage, I feel closest to my wife and most in love when we've spent time together, talking and understanding each other's heart. The same goes for me and Jesus. And in both cases, words don't actually have to be spoken for meaning to come through.

As the minister read my providential tribute at Ted's funeral, I resolved to never ignore that still small voice again, but to obey it – even if God asked me to do something far outside of my comfort zone.

I left Ted's ceremony with a clear understanding that God would continue to use me as long as I made myself available. I don't believe that God only uses "super-Christians" or some pedigreed "chosen" people. I believe he uses anyone whose heart is surrendered to him, and whoever earns his trust by responding to his voice.

○   ○   ○

"Love the Lord... listen to his voice and hold fast to him. For the Lord is your life, and he will give you many years in the land..." (Deuteronomy 30:20)

11

HYDRANT:
Unquenchable Thirst

Hollywood history is full of famous movie stars with unforgettable names. Names that will live on forever. Names like Archibald Leach, Marion Morrison, and Norma Mortensen. If you're drawing a blank, don't feel bad. You probably know these Oscar winners better as Cary Grant, John Wayne, and Marilyn Monroe.

Scores of celebrities have changed their names to advance their careers, including Bernard Schwarz (Tony Curtis), Maurice Micklewhite (Michael Caine), and Betty Joan Perske (Lauren Bacall). Some did it to disguise their ethnicity, like Dino Crocetti (Dean Martin). Some did it for artistic effect, like Louise Ciccone (Madonna). Others simply did it to leave room on the marquee for co-stars, like Goldie Jean Studlendegehawn (Goldie Hawn).

But entertainers aren't the only ones who've benefited from name changes. Adolf Hitler would have had trouble getting crowds to chant "Heil Schicklgruber!" And Joseph

Stalin would not have seemed quite so menacing if he had stuck with the moniker Iosif Vissarionovich Dzhugashvilli.

Even the Bible has its share of name changes. At the tender age of 99, the founder of the Hebrew nation had his name changed by God himself from Abram ("exalted father") to Abraham ("father of many"). In the same chapter of Genesis, we see God also change the name of Abraham's wife from Sarai ("contentious") to Sarah ("princess").

Fast forward 900 years: The beloved apostle who wrote two-thirds of the New Testament is best known to us as Paul. But our first glimpse of him is not as Paul the preacher, but as Saul the persecutor. Furious at the new Christian sect, Rabbi Saul zealously tried to stamp them out of existence by arresting and imprisoning them. The earliest mention of Saul (Acts 7:54-58) finds him on hand for the stoning of the church's first martyr, Stephen. Some think he may have even been in charge of the execution.

After his dramatic conversion on the road to Damascus (Acts 9), Saul became better known as Paul and spread the gospel over the entire known world until his death by beheading in A.D. 68. Along the way, he took time out to mentor and train a young believer named Timothy with advice like: *"Don't let anyone look down on you because you are young, but set an example for the believers in speech, in life, in faith, and in purity"* (1 Timothy 4:12).

Paul worked unselfishly with Timothy, developing his spiritual gifts and encouraging him to use them: *"Until I come, devote yourself to the public reading of Scripture, to preaching and to teaching. Do not neglect your gift…"* (1 Timothy 4:13-14).

Like Timothy, I was a young believer who needed a "Paul" – a mature Christian willing to pour himself into my life. Someone gentle enough to love me when I failed, but strong enough to kick me in the pants when I got lazy.

Somebody smart enough to teach me, but humble enough not to lord his knowledge over me. Early in my spiritual journey, God brought just such a man into my life.

I first met "my Paul" at a workshop he taught called *24/7 With Jesus*. His name was Craig, and he was a teaching pastor at Kensington. At first, we were just acquaintances, but our paths kept crossing in unusual ways. Because he was a friend of a friend, Craig would occasionally sit in on our men's small group. He never said much during our lessons, preferring to let us figure out our own application of Bible truth. But when he did choose to speak, it pretty much blew us away. Not only was he a highly educated Bible scholar and deep thinker, but this Ph.D. was as humble and gentle in spirit as any man I'd ever met.

After working at Kensington for a year, Craig "coincidentally" moved his family to within a few miles of where I lived. In fact, his home was so close to ours that my son and I helped him move in. I thought it was strange that he would relocate so far from the church, but was excited that I now had easy access to my new friend.

Because of his association with my men's group, I called on Craig to help out with the funeral for Pat's husband. After hearing the story of how God used me in Pat's life, Craig began to understand my heart and passion for Jesus. He could tell I was thirsty for God, and he began to "fill my cup" to test my response. The result? The more I drank, the thirstier I became.

Before we came to know each other well, we had an unusual encounter while my family was spending a week vacationing in northern Michigan. One night, we drove into the town of Elk Rapids for dinner. When the meal was over, we waited for the check, but service was slow. The kids were getting antsy and worried they were going to miss the only movie in town. To keep the peace, Gina decided to drive them over and come back to pick me up.

After paying the bill, I stepped outside to the street and sat down on the curb to wait. The sun was setting, the birds were singing, and a soft breeze stirred the flowers lining the quiet street. I relaxed there with my arms over my knees and my head resting in my arms, completely enjoying my time alone.

Suddenly, out of the corner of my eye, I saw the figure of a man running toward me. Turning, I could see him waving his arms and yelling my name. Surprised, I looked up to see my friend Craig bounding over. Winded from his sprint, he blurted, "Jeff! Are you OK?!"

In shock, I mumbled, "I'm fine. But what in the world are you doing here?"

Catching his breath, Craig explained that his parents had a place on nearby Crystal Lake and his family was up visiting. He was driving into Elk Rapids to see one of his brothers when he spotted me hunched over on the side of the road and slammed on the brakes. He said I had looked depressed and lost. And what in the world was I doing way up here anyway? And why was I was alone? When I told him I was just waiting for Gina to return, he finally calmed down. To this day we still laugh about his rescue.

Later, when we were recalling the incident, I told him my father had grown up on Crystal Lake in the small lakeshore town of Beulah, and that I used to spend my summers there in the early 1970s with my grandparents. I shared stories of blissful summer days swimming, fishing, and occasionally teasing the locals with practical jokes.

Not to be outdone, Craig told me a funny story about how he and his brothers pulled a boyhood prank he had never forgotten. One lazy day in August, the three boys dreamed up a scheme that called for courage and nerves of steel: In broad daylight and without masks, the boys would ride their bikes right through the biggest store in downtown Beulah.

As he described their daring antics, my eyes opened wide in disbelief. I told him I also remembered that story – because my grandparents owned the store! It was called "Petherick's Five and Dime" and I often worked there as a boy. In fact, I was actually on duty at the candy counter the day Craig's posse wheeled in. For some unknown reason, my grandparents thought they could trust their 8-year-old grandson not to gorge himself in the midst of unlimited free candy. They were wrong. Surrounded by so much sugary temptation, I managed to do a pretty good job of measuring out candy for customers, but felt I was entitled to a bag of my own each time someone came in.

My sweet tooth aside, I clearly remembered the day the boys rode their bicycles into the store. They brazenly rode through the front doors and pedaled down one aisle and back up the other and right out the door. My grandpa was too stunned to move. Sensing he was not happy about the wheeled visitors, I suppressed my urge to cheer them on. Until the day gramps died, he tried to figure out who the mystery riders were. He knew nearly everyone in the small town, but he did not recognize these "hoodlums." Little did he know that one of the delinquents would grow up to be a pastor!

Because of our similar backgrounds and interests, we soon formed a bond of friendship. I sensed early on, however, that God brought Craig into my life for more than just hanging out together. There were far too many coincidences for our relationship not to be a divine appointment. Because I was being pulled into incidents like Ted's death more and more frequently, I wanted to understand God and Scripture in a deeper way.

Sucking up my courage, I asked Craig if he would consider being my personal spiritual trainer. He agreed, I exhaled, and we began meeting regularly for breakfast. Much of the time, Craig would just sit and quietly listen like he used to in our men's group. But when he did speak, it would inevitably reveal some truth about God that I needed to hear. My faith (and my waistline) grew with every meeting. Although I read and studied on my own, it was these one-on-one meetings with Craig that accelerated my growth. Knowing I was a voracious reader, he gave me an endless list of thought-provoking books by the great Christian authors.

I often wondered why Craig had agreed to spend so much time with me. After all, I knew how busy he was as a pastor and teacher. I figured if he was going to mentor anyone, it would be a "professional Christian" – someone committed to serving Jesus in full-time ministry. Why waste his valuable time on an ordinary guy-next-door believer? Why mentor a man who worked in Wall Street finance instead of religion?

As grateful as I was for his time and attention, the question nagged at me. It bothered me so much I finally asked him one morning over breakfast. Putting down his fork, Craig explained how he had sensed God stirring in his heart to pour into someone, just as Paul poured his life into Timothy. Then he said, "If I've heard anything clearly from God about you, it's this – at some point in your life, God is going to call you to something very different than what you're currently doing. But before God can do that, he needs to strengthen your character and faith."

Craig pledged to help me in that process.

I drove home from that breakfast in tears, not because of the hot sauce, but because I had recently felt the same prompting from God. Craig's comment confirmed to me that I was hearing the Lord correctly.

On a business trip to Seattle just weeks before, I had stopped in to visit some close friends who had recently moved west. Strong Christians, they were two of the many seed-planters who spoke truth into our lives before Gina and I surrendered to Jesus. Now, my passion was invigorating their walk. As I was leaving, Steve and Amy handed me a copy of *Halftime* by Bob Buford. I devoured it cover to cover during the plane ride home, and it spoke directly to what I was experiencing.

Buford writes that the first half of life is all about achieving success as measured by the world's definition. We want the money and the nice house, and we're willing to work hard to earn them. But when we reach midlife, we look around at all of our accomplishments and possessions and like Peggy Lee, we wonder, *Is that all there is?*

For many, this empty feeling triggers a quest for something else to fill the hole: a hobby, a Harley, an affair, whatever. This is the vulnerable tipping point that Buford calls "halftime," the period when what we are *really* searching for is significance. At our very core, we all want our lives to mean more than earthly possessions and social status. Jesus asked, *"What good is it for a man to gain the whole world, yet forfeit his soul?"* (Mark 8:36).

Once again I felt the hand of God guiding me to the exact truth I needed. It now seemed clear that he was preparing me for a life of significance, not success. At first I wanted to jumpstart God's plan, to race ahead of his timing. But as Buford suggests, halftime can be a short period for regrouping and rethinking, or it can be a much longer window of time, as God moves and prepares us for major change. Although I was impatient at first, I realized my preparation would probably be lengthy. Instead of obsessing with knowing where God was taking me, I decided to relax and enjoy the ride.

Craig's answer to me that morning brought a new perspective to my life. I had certainly felt God moving in me, but I was confused and unsure of what he wanted from me. Through Craig's discernment, I saw that what God wanted most from me was my surrendered and obedient heart. Why? Because if he could *trust* me, he could *use* me. To be sure, he started me out with the little things: phone calls, letter writing, and sharing my experience with others. But I knew that if I were *"faithful with a few things"* God would put me *"in charge of many things"* (Mathew 25:21).

Today, I have peace in knowing that when God calls me, I will be ready to go (sometimes enthusiastically, sometimes kicking and screaming) wherever he sends me. That could mean continuing to touch lives as a businessman, or handing out bags of rice in India, or standing behind a pulpit, or working with teens, or raising funds for AIDS victims. Or something altogether different. All I know is that I can trust God with my future, and whatever his plan is for me, it promises a richer and more rewarding life than anything I could ever come up with.

Craig and I continue to meet, and I am grateful for him in my life. At times I feel like Timothy must have felt, honored to have someone as knowledgeable and passionate as Paul (or Craig) pouring into his life. The relationship, however, has now shifted to a two-way street – my curiosity about God leads to many thoughtful discussions that reveal a deeper understanding to both of us.

I don't know how long "halftime" will be for me. I've stopped trying to figure that out. I'm simply trusting that when God speaks, I will listen and respond. And I know that God has put Craig in my life to make sure the game plan I come up with for the second half is a page out of God's own playbook: *"But you, man of God, flee from all this, and pursue righteousness, godliness, faith, love, endurance and gentleness. Fight the good fight of faith"* (1 Timothy 6:11-12).

Now, if he would just consider changing his name. I mean, if Herbert Buckingham Khaury can become Tiny Tim, why can't Craig become Paul?

12

CONFIRMATION:
God Unplugged

If you're feeling drowsy right about now, I'm not offended.

After all, it's estimated that nearly 50 percent of all adults are sleep deprived. We owe this unhappy trend to longer work days, increased commuting times, and the stress of our around-the-clock society.

You've probably heard that the average person spends a third of his life sleeping. But do we? The National Sleep Foundation says the average American only sleeps 6 hours and 58 minutes a night. Before Thomas Edison invented the light bulb, we averaged nine hours. Which is right in the sweet spot of the eight to ten hours experts say we need to stay healthy.

We're so chronically tired that one-third of all drivers will fall asleep behind the wheel at least once during their lifetime. And countless tragedies have been blamed on exhaustion, including the Exxon Valdez oil spill, the Challenger shuttle disaster, and the Chernobyl nuclear accident. Not to mention really grouchy co-workers.

To make things worse, the normal slumber we take for granted as a kid becomes much tougher to achieve as an adult. So tough that Americans spend $2.2 billion a year on sleeping pills. Plus millions more for sleep clinics, hypnosis, and acupuncture. When counting sheep fails, some of us spend up to $3,000 for an adjustable mattress. If the sandman goes AWOL, others opt for bedside sound effects with their choice of babbling brooks, ocean waves, or chirping crickets.

With millions of weary people begging for rest, why would anyone in their right mind voluntarily get up one hour earlier than they had to? That's the question I ask myself every time my bare feet hit the cold floor of my dark bedroom.

The answer, of course, is Dewey.

○　　○　　○

My early morning time with God was starting to become a consistent part of my life. I noticed that the days when I skipped my heavenly chat room were never quite as peaceful or productive as the days that began centered on Jesus. It also seemed that my morning devotions were helping me hear from God more regularly.

Often the promptings were about things that needed improvement in my own life. For example, God pointed out that I had not been the most patient father or most affirming husband. He reminded me I was often critical and judgmental of others, especially my kids. I worried about my business too much. I was not a great listener. I left the toilet seat up (sorry, that was my wife speaking). The point is, just when I thought I was getting the whole "Christ-like" thing going, God was up early to reveal something else in me that needed work.

In the winter, my morning prayer time was spent in the basement, with the door closed and the gas fireplace turned on. It's the quietest part of the house, and if I get up before the kids get ready for school, I can keep my undivided focus on God. It's cozy, but after a long Michigan winter, cabin fever sets in and I'm ready to get outside. Always a nature lover, I grew up spending my summers in northern Michigan at Crystal Lake and along the Au Sable River. Fishing, hiking, and hunting, I learned to appreciate the outdoors as a child, and it's still where I'm happiest as an adult. So when it's warm enough to pray outdoors, I head for the deck that overlooks the narrow, winding pond in front of our house. In the quiet beauty of nature, it's easy to feel God's presence around me as I read and pray.

One morning in late fall, I was sitting on my deck praying, when I heard the distinct whisper of God. For some reason, God put a friend named Dewey on my heart. It was such a powerful interruption that I knew instantly it was a prompting by God. After my experience with Ted, I had learned to recognize the difference between God's voice and my own thoughts. So I rushed into work that morning with a burning desire to contact Dewey immediately.

Dewey was a member of my men's group, and as far as I knew, there was nothing unusual going on in his life. Like me, he had given his life to Jesus just a few years earlier. In fact, before we knew each other, we were actually baptized on the same day at the same baptism service. Dewey's passion to know Jesus was infectious. Even though he was 15 years older than me and in a totally different season of life, we felt like young brothers going through the same experience together. The change in Dewey was fun to watch, as slowly but surely, he surrendered his heart and life to Jesus.

Every guy in my men's group felt a special bond to Dewey. In the ways of the world he was like a father to us, but in the ways of Christianity he was still a child. With so much to learn, he was like a human sponge, trying to soak it all up as fast as possible. His enthusiasm inspired all of us to go deeper in our relationship with Jesus.

I practically ran into my office that morning and immediately logged onto my computer to locate Dewey's phone number. Frustrated, I searched everywhere, but couldn't find it. Then I remembered leaving it inside my men's group study book. Unfortunately, I couldn't call home for it because my wife Gina had an early morning meeting at church.

I was stumped.

Half praying, half complaining, I asked God for help fulfilling his request. Suddenly, in the middle of a rant, I recalled that Dewey had sent me an e-mail earlier in the week. I pulled up my archives and found his address. Hurriedly, I typed out a message: "Dewey, for some reason God put you on my heart this morning and I feel like I am supposed to talk with you. I forgot your number at home, so when you get this, please give me a call at work."

I clicked "send" at 8:15 a.m. and fully expected to get an immediate reply. Instead, I got nothing but spam. Hours dragged by with no response. I waited in my office, but heard nothing from him all day. I began wondering if he had even received the e-mail, so I checked to make sure it was sent by the system. Nothing was wrong with our server, so I assumed he must have gone out of town. By the end of the day, darker thoughts emerged: *What if Dewey had actually received my message, concluded I was nuts, and decided not to call me back?*

At home that night, I wondered why God had so clearly asked me to get in touch with Dewey and then denied me the opportunity. Knowing I would see Dewey at our next men's group in a few days, I decided to wait until then to ask him about that morning. Maybe my question would spark something in his mind that would make sense of why God placed him on my heart. Content that I would eventually find out, I was finally able to sleep.

Next morning, I returned to work. Before I could take my jacket off, the phone rang. Surprised by such an early call, I picked it up.

It was Dewey, but he didn't sound like his usual jovial self. He actually sounded a bit hostile and confrontational. Without bothering to say good morning, he jumped right into the conversation.

"Why did you send me that e-mail yesterday?" he blurted. I was taken aback by his abrupt question, and it took me a few seconds to respond.

"Well, I felt like God put you on my heart during my prayer time. Is something going on?" I asked.

He paused for a long moment and then asked, "Do you have any idea what Joan and I did yesterday?"

"No," I said. "I have no idea."

"Joan and I locked the doors to our house, took the phone off the hook, and closed all the shades on the windows," he said. "And then we prayed all day to God. At the end of the day, we were certain that we had heard clearly from him that we are supposed to leave Michigan and move to Salt Lake City with the Kensington church-planting team."

My jaw dropped in amazement.

Once again, I was caught off guard by God's love for his people. I told Dewey that God had used me to send a message of encouragement and affirmation to him and his wife. Dewey agreed. He said that when he opened my belated e-mail, he got tears in his eyes as he realized exactly what it represented. He said my e-mail was part of the confirmation that they indeed heard God's calling correctly.

I hung up the phone in awe. I wondered what would have happened if I had somehow found Dewey's phone number. Would I have left the same message? Would I have just waited to call him back? It didn't matter. The e-mail was clear evidence of God's overwhelming love.

Six months later, our men's group gathered to say goodbye to Dewey at a special lunch in his honor. After reminiscing about the ways God had moved in our lives, we gathered around a table with bread and wine to take communion. Then, arm in arm, we prayed for Dewey and Joan and their incredible journey with God. There wasn't a dry eye in the group. I was so choked up I could barely get through my prayer of dedication.

It seemed amazing that this man – a spiritual baby just a few short years ago – was boldly following God to an unknown place for an unknown purpose. Watching him uproot and relocate was a living example of the kind of faith we all longed for in our group. We were so proud of Dewey and certain he was going to make a huge impact in Utah.

Dewey's story reinforced for me how much the Father loves his children. He is always there when we take a step of faith; to encourage us and let us know we're headed in the right direction. When we pray and seek God's will, he will eventually get through to us – somehow – to let us know how we fit into his plan.

As Dewey proved, when we honor God privately behind closed doors, he makes his presence known publicly: *"But when you pray, go into your room, close the door and pray to your Father, who is unseen. Then your Father who sees what is done in secret, will reward you"* (Mathew 6:6).

13

GIVING:
This Changes Everything

Elijah Wood's been there. Orlando Bloom's been there. Liv Tyler, Viggo Mortensen, and Christopher Lee, too. But chances are that you've never set foot there.

If you haven't guessed, I'm talking about New Zealand, the real-life "Middle Earth" where director Peter Jackson filmed the Tolkien trilogy *Lord of the Rings.* With geographic diversity ranging from snow-capped mountains to hot springs, it was easy for Jackson to transform the stunning landscapes into the elf city of Rivendell, the rolling hills of Hobbiton, and the alpine fortress of Rohan.

Home to just 4 million residents, New Zealand is an unspoiled country where sheep outnumber people 15 to 1. And it's a country where you can enjoy both world class snow skiing and spectacular surfing at places like Shipwreck Bay (named by none other than Captain Cook). In fact, New Zealand's slopes and beaches have been rated among the world's most beautiful. But for one young surfer, the call to serve God was louder than the lure of ocean waves crashing on Mahia Peninsula.

As a free-spirited teenager, Nadine lived from one wild party to the next. Her crowd was fast and her celebrity friends included actors, musicians, and sports stars. But the thrills of surfing and the glamour of the club scene left her empty inside. Searching for the perfect wave or the perfect party grew tiring. Her mother was a woman of strong faith, and by prayer and patience she reached through the wall of indifference Nadine had built around herself.

After years of dealing with the painful consequences of bad choices, Nadine finally gave her life to Jesus. A young woman with a new focus, she was eager to hear God's truth and move past her mistakes.

Ironically, just as the mother-daughter bond was being cemented again, Nadine felt called to leave her native New Zealand and work as a counselor at a Christian youth camp in Maryland. At age 19, she flew 6,000 miles to endure a summer of eating hot dogs, swatting mosquitoes, and singing Kumbya. When the camp ended, a friend introduced her to the leaders of a church in Imlay City, Michigan. She wound up spending the next eight weeks helping out as a volunteer in their youth ministry.

Her visit was cut short when she injured her knee playing basketball. She returned to New Zealand to recuperate, spend time with family, and finish her degree. Like all "kiwis," she was thrilled to be home, but the church in Michigan was begging her to come back. She returned in December 1998 – this time to work for the church. Because of the church sponsorship, the U.S. government granted her a three-year R1 religious visa. While there, she lived with a couple who volunteered to share their home. "Coincidently," the homeowner's nephew, Mark, just happened to be Director of the Arts at Kensington

Church where we were attending. Eventually, Nadine met Mark. A year later, when Nadine felt called to leave her job as Youth Pastor at the Imlay City church, Mark offered her a position on the Arts Team at Kensington.

Nadine accepted the offer, but there was one major problem: Because she switched employers, her visa status changed, and it would be some time before Kensington could sponsor her. Since Canada is part of the British Commonwealth (like New Zealand), she decided to visit Ontario and return on a tourist visa.

So far so good. But re-entering the U.S. as a tourist created another major problem – Kensington could not legally pay her. Undeterred, Nadine worked at Kensington for free for two-and-a-half years. Receiving zero wages, she survived through the generosity of kind people God brought into her life. She lived with a girlfriend, Toni, in a tiny apartment where they shared the same bedroom. Living by faith, she was grateful to those who helped her, but often felt like a burden. She prayed that someday she could support herself and find a place of her own. The upside of being perpetually broke was learning to trust God at a new level. She was confident the big hand of God was all over her life as she witnessed his daily provision.

Never in her life had she been so dependent on God for the bare essentials. Or so sure of his reliability: *"So do not worry, saying, 'What shall we eat?' or 'What shall we drink?' or 'What shall we wear?" For the pagans run after all these things, and your heavenly Father knows that you need them. But seek first his kingdom and his righteousness, and all these things will be given to you as well"* (Matthew 6:31-33).

In December 2001, Kensington showed a video about Nadine's faith journey. Her dramatic testimony touched my wife and me deeply. We had never seen anyone with so much trust that God would take care of them. On top of that, she seemed so happy and grateful for the bare-bones lifestyle she was living.

Her contentment helped us put our own lives into perspective. We repented of ever having been ungrateful, or envious of others, or wasting time worrying about things we didn't have. Nadine's example helped us to appreciate how God had richly provided for our family in incredible ways.

Nadine's visa troubles continued into 2002. Things looked bleak. At one point, the government actually asked her to leave. She tried to explain that she was serving another church and deserved a religious visa, but nothing worked. Meanwhile, the Kensington Arts Team prayed daily for a miracle that would allow her to stay.

With deportation looming, she decided to try an outrageous scheme. It involved what on the surface appeared to be a sightseeing trip with her co-worker, Dan, and his teenage nephew, Mitch. Packed into a rented Chevy Impala, they drove westward to Yellowstone and Glacier National Parks. Finally, it was time to put the plan into action. Packing up their camping gear, they headed north to Banff, Canada. The plan was simple but risky. If she came back into the U.S. through this extremely remote border crossing, maybe she would get a sympathetic Customs Agent. Dan, who was also on the Arts Team, was carrying an official letter from Kensington management stating that they would sponsor her on a R1 visa.

As they approached the border crossing, they pulled the car to the side of the road. Surrounded by the awesome beauty of the Rocky Mountains, they prayed that God would soften the heart of the agent that Nadine would face. They prayed that God would go before them and clear any obstacles: *"I lift up my eyes to the hills – where does my help come from? My help comes from the Lord, the Maker of heaven and earth"* (Psalm 121:1-2).

Hearts pounding, they pulled up to the Montana border check station and told Nadine's story. The guard asked them to get out of the vehicle and step inside the building to talk to an agent. It was a woman, and she seemed new in the job. As she moved through the process, the rookie agent went back and forth between the desk and her supervisor for well over an hour. Nadine was unsure what was happening, and was anxious about her shaky situation. Praying silently, she vowed that whatever the outcome, she would accept it as God's will. But for her part, she felt called to Kensington. Her heart was there, and this unlikely group of turned-on believers had truly become her family. Finally, after an agonizing two-hour wait, the agent returned with a one-year visa. With the clunk of a rubber stamp, Nadine was heading back to her home away from home.

After many tears and warm embraces, the three travelers started back to Michigan, where Nadine could finally begin earning a living. God had miraculously given her valuable time to work out a more permanent solution.

In the summer of 2002, Nadine began working with Kensington's high school ministry called "edge." In addition to programming responsibilities for their arts program, she agreed to become a small group coach for high school students. At the same time, I believed God was calling me to the high school ministry as a small group leader. With two teens of our own, Gina and I decided to open up our home for the weekly youth meetings. We figured with two acres of land, an outdoor fire pit, and a spacious family room, it would be the perfect site for teenagers. Shortly after offering the use of our home, we found out that Nadine would be our "house coach."

We were excited. We had never met Nadine in person, but we had been so impacted by her story we couldn't wait to welcome her. We knew she would be an incredibly positive influence on the students, especially our own children.

That fall, Nadine started working with a dozen or so students at our house. Every Sunday night, Nadine led the large group time and proved to be a gifted leader and role model. The boys in the group were a little unruly and immature, and many times I just sat back and marveled at how Nadine patiently and gracefully handled them. Harnessing the energy of teenage boys is a lot like herding cats, but the love of Jesus was evident in her smile and kind demeanor. Many times, she captivated them with stories of her life, sharing mistakes she had made, and how God is able to use our brokenness for his glory. Examples of how God had supernaturally provided for her during difficult times were especially moving.

During the course of our weekly meetings, Gina and I grew closer to Nadine. Sometimes, after the students left, we would sit and talk for hours about God and life. One evening in November, we were talking about the remodeling project that was transforming the outbuilding on our property into a functional guesthouse. It was almost finished, and we were talking with Gina's grandmother, Nan, about moving in. During the conversation, Nadine mentioned that she was finally earning some money, and was eager to move out of the cramped apartment she was sharing. She liked our area and asked us to let her know if we saw anything come up for rent.

The following week, Gina got some bad news about her grandmother. At age 82, Nan had taken a turn for the worse, and her forgetfulness had just been diagnosed as dementia. In her new condition, Nan wouldn't be able to live in the guesthouse.

We were sad and confused. Why would God prompt us to create a guesthouse if Nan was not healthy enough to live there? Then one day while praying, God brought Nadine to mind. Alone in my prayer time, I thought to myself, *Maybe it was Nadine that God had in mind all along when he told us to finish the guest house.*

When we asked Nadine if she would like to live there, she was ecstatic. For months, she had passed by it every time we walked down to the fire pit with the students. Like me, she loved nature and looked forward to the peace and quiet the guesthouse would offer. We thanked God for clarity and began counting the days.

The construction was finished in November, and Gina and I spent December happily furnishing it for Nadine.

That January, Nadine went on a mission trip to Africa with a Kensington team. Being in Kenya with the primitive Pokot tribe was an amazing experience for her, but the most astounding part of the trip happened upon her return. Once again, she had to re-enter through U.S. customs and would be interrogated about her visa. Unfortunately, it would be expiring in less than six months. She knew it was risky leaving the country again, but she felt it was God's calling to go on the African mission. Whatever happened, she felt comforted in knowing that he would guide her through the red tape and bureaucratic quagmire.

Landing at Detroit's international terminal, the exhausted missions team approached the customs area. With our senior pastor, Steve, ahead of her, and our teaching pastor, Dave, behind her, Nadine walked toward customs. The lines were long and the waiting seemed to take forever. Inching forward, the entire team was praying. When she stepped into the booth, the agent looked at her current visa, but for reasons God only knows, did not notice the stack of previous visas behind it. This just doesn't happen, folks. It was a true blue miracle and then it got better: He stamped her current visa and gave her four more years in the United States.

Nadine returned to the newly finished guesthouse, and

unpacked in a place she could finally call her own. Naturally, there were a few bumps in the road and occasional awkward moments until we all got used to the living arrangements. For the first year, we worked on establishing boundaries to ensure harmony between us. I'm sure there were times when she felt more like a tenant than a friend. But as time went on, a bond of family love formed between us, and we shared holidays, dinners, and funny stories.

For instance, none of us will ever forget the time I defended Nadine against a huge, enormous, gigantic bat (did I mention it was big?). The evil monster had flown into her house and threatened to suck out her blood at any moment. Armed with a fire poker, a broom, and a fishing net, I represented my entire gender with cunning, skill, and a hunter's instinct. My display of macho bravery against a frightened one-ounce fruit bat is still a source of laughter (and derision).

In many ways, Nadine has become a member of our family. To our teens, she has become a big sister, especially to our daughter Kira. To Gina and me, she is both a friend and a second daughter, and we can't help feeling parental in our responsibility to her. Frankly, we're thrilled that she calls us her American family.

Gina and I know we are blessed, and feel constantly challenged to be good stewards of the financial resources God's given us. When we were brand new believers, we felt guilty about our material possessions. We wondered if we needed to give them all away to truly follow Jesus. But as we matured, God revealed that what really mattered to him was not our possessions, but our hearts – whether we were investing in earthly things or in heavenly things: *"Do not store up for yourselves treasures on earth... But store up for yourselves treasures in heaven, where moth and rust do not destroy, and where thieves do not break in and steal. For where your treasure is, there your heart will be also"* (Matthew 6:19-21).

The guesthouse was an important lesson. It sat empty and unused for too long. Neglected, it was only a nuisance with no real value to anyone. But when we gave it away, our family life was enriched beyond our dreams: *"Give and it will be given to you"* (Luke 6:38).

For Nadine, the unexpected guesthouse helped her realize how much God loved and cared for her. It strengthened her faith to see that the God who owns everything everywhere cares about her individual daily needs: *"Cast all your anxiety on him because he cares for you"* (1 Peter 5:7).

For Gina and me, sharing the guesthouse helped us understand that people – not things – matter to God. If we're willing to use our resources to help people, God will often prompt us to take action, like opening our homes and our wallets. If we're willing to be God's pipeline, he will bless others through us. Sharing what we've been given is liberating, exhilarating, and a little scary.

But it is not optional.

○   ○   ○

"From everyone who has been given much, much will be demanded; and from the one who has been entrusted with much, much more will be asked." (Luke 12:48)

14

HOPƐ:
Higher Ways

Moving 300 miles per hour, the 50-foot-high wall of water slammed into the coastline like a battering ram. When the huge wave receded, it sucked entire towns and villages back into the ocean, leaving bare sand where cites had been standing moments earlier.

Estimates vary, but the tsunami that struck December 26, 2004 killed at least 225,000 people in India, Indonesia, and Thailand. Causing mass destruction in 11 countries, the largest disaster in modern times left almost as many questions as casualties: What triggered it? Could it have been predicted? Will it happen again?

Beyond the questions for scientists and seismologists, people were asking clergy even tougher questions: Did God cause it? If not, why didn't he prevent it? Was it a judgment against an evil world?

Answers and opinions ran the gamut, but one thing was certain – the tsunami killed without regard to race, religion, or creed. Muslims, Christians, and Buddhists died side by side. Tourists and terrorists. Pastors and pimps. Cops and criminals all drowned together. This equal opportunity killer begged the question: Why do bad things happen to good people?

In my life, this question went from hypothetical to up-close-and-personal on one unforgettable afternoon in March 2003. Our seventh-grade daughter, Kira, walked in from school and slumped in a chair. She was visibly upset. Trembling, she told us terrible news – her friend Katie* had just been diagnosed with cancer.

We were heartbroken. When Kira was emotionally troubled, Katie was the only girl on the school bus who invited Kira to sit with her. Kira was not only the new kid in school, but had a rough time making friends because of her uncontrollable outbursts and anger. It took a unique and loving person to reach out to such an outcast – especially one shunned by the "cool" kids. Although she was pretty and popular herself, Katie never worried about who was "in" or "out." She genuinely cared about everyone, regardless of social standing. Kira never forgot how Katie stood by her in the dark lonely days, and she was hit hard by her friend's illness.

The day I surrendered my life to God, I promised I would do whatever he asked me to from that point on. As a spiritual novice, I assumed he would start me out with a few simple requests and work up from there. If I were obedient in the little things, he would steadily increase my responsibilities: *"Whoever can be trusted with very little can also be trusted with much"* (Luke 16:10).

Even in the Old Testament, those who served God with high impact were allowed to tackle small tasks first: David faithfully tended his dad's sheep before tending Israel as king. He killed wolves in the pasture before killing Goliath

*Not her real name.

on the battlefield. Moses followed goats around the foothills of Midian for 14,240 long hot days before encountering the burning bush on Mount Sinai. A former prince of Egypt, Moses wore out his royal Birkenstocks stepping around cow pies for 40 years before God felt he was ready to handle the Super Bowl of really hard stuff to do – leading 6 million slaves away from the all-powerful pharaoh.

Based on these and other Biblical examples, my strategy was for God to start me out easy – write a letter, call a friend, fix up a house – then gradually turn up the heat. That day in March, God ditched my plan and spun the thermostat to blowtorch level.

Katie's cancer began as a lump on her jawbone. When she complained that the side of her face was hurting, her primary care physician dismissed it as nothing to worry about. Thankfully, her parents did their own research and took her to a hospital specializing in pediatric cancer. The doctors there confirmed she had developed a rare form of cancer in her jaw. Because of its unusual location, they could not operate on the tumor. They would have to treat it with radiation and radical chemotherapy.

Kira asked if I would pray for Katie during my morning prayer time.

I began praying for Katie the next day. As usual, my prayers felt inadequate. I never knew how to begin, and I was never exactly sure what to ask for. I prayed for general things like strength, peace, and comfort for the family during this difficult time. I also prayed that Katie would have the stamina to get through the 42 weeks of chemo treatments she would have to endure. My heart was in the right place, but Katie was just one name on my long list of generalized requests.

Later, I told Katie's story to my friend Craig during our weekly meeting. Over breakfast and coffee, he told me to start getting more specific in my prayers. I had always felt like that was too pushy – too much to expect from a busy God. I had always felt selfish asking for specific needs. But Craig reminded me how personal God is, and how he loves it when we present our detailed requests to him. Would I ask our waitress to just "bring me food" or "bring me two eggs over easy with blueberry pancakes"?

Craig reminded me of a favorite passage: *"Do not be anxious about anything, but in everything, by prayer and petition, with thanksgiving, present your requests to God"* (Philippians 4:6).

The following Thursday, I began to get very specific. With no apologies, I asked God pointblank to heal Katie. On my knees, I petitioned him to let his divine hands touch her face with his healing power and make the cancer disappear. Then I simply listened. Previous "divine moments" had taught me that I should expect a two-way conversation with God. While I certainly didn't hear God's whisper every time I prayed, I heard it enough to know I should be listening intently.

That morning he spoke clearly. God's thoughts penetrated my quietness, and I heard him say, *Go to her in person and pray. I need you to be my instrument.*

Obviously, there had been a mistake.

Or maybe I hadn't heard him correctly. Or maybe it was just my own thoughts bouncing around my head. Whatever the snafu, I dismissed the idea completely. There was no way God would ask me to do this. I hardly knew Katie, let alone her parents. And while Gina and Katie's mom at least chatted whenever the kids played, I was clueless.

Certainly I was not the instrument God was looking for.

By this point in my journey, I had experienced God stirring my heart many times before. But this time I completely disobeyed his prompting. Instead, I spent my time and energy coming up with rational, plausible, sensible excuses why it could not have been his voice.

The following morning, I was back in Scripture and prayer. My curiosity about healing was sky high and I eagerly read the Bible story where Jesus sent out his disciples two-by-two into the surrounding towns and villages. Empowered by his Holy Spirit, the formerly inept disciples performed amazing acts of healing throughout the countryside (Luke 9:1-6).

Again, I prayed for God to heal Katie – to reach down from heaven with his invisible hand to touch her face and heal her. Energized by studying scripture, I was more specific with God than ever.

In response, he was more specific with me.

His unmistakable reply was, *I'm not there to do that, but you can do it for me. I want you to go and pray for Katie, and I want you to place your left hand on her cheek and pray for healing.*

This time, I knew whose voice it was and I freaked out. I stopped praying immediately and began to weep uncontrollably. I was so overtaken by the power of the Holy Spirit that I just broke down and cried.

Stunned at hearing God so clearly, I was overcome with equal parts turmoil and fear. I had promised God I would be obedient to him "whatever, whenever, wherever," and I knew I had no choice. But I couldn't help wondering how I was going to pull this off without Katie's parents thinking I was nuts. If I told them "God spoke to me" they'd think I was crazy. If I said "God wants to use me to heal Katie," they'd think I was insane. No way would they let a deranged man near their precious daughter. And who could blame them? Even I was beginning to think I was losing it.

I left my basement den and went upstairs to get ready for work. I continued crying as I showered that morning. Shaving, crying, brushing, crying – I could not get hold of myself. Gina heard me sobbing and wondered what was wrong. I told her what had just happened in my prayer time; how I knew I had no choice in the matter, and how I had no idea how to arrange this potentially awkward meeting. I think she was scared too, but she just hugged me and encouraged me that if this was God's will, it would happen.

On the way to work, I listened to worship music and the tears continued nonstop. But as I inched through rush-hour traffic, I began to feel a new peace. God was whispering, *Don't worry. I will work it out for you.*

The next morning, Gina called Katie's mom to set up a play date with the two girls. Kira had been asking if she could see Katie to offer her encouragement. In the middle of the conversation, Gina felt a stirring in her heart to mention what had happened to me the previous morning in prayer.

This disclosure was totally unplanned.

As she told Katie's mom the story, she was pleased and surprised by her openness to the idea. Katie's parents had also been praying and asking for a miracle. So far so good. But as she listened, Gina sensed bitterness creeping into the mother's voice. Then, she asked the ultimate question: "Why Katie? She is such a sweet and kind little girl. Why would God do something like this to her?"

Gina gently explained that God did not inflict Katie with cancer, but that he could and would bring something good out of even the worst of circumstances. "Maybe Jeff is part of that plan," she said, reminding her of the promise in Romans 8:28, *"And we know that in all things God works for the good of those who love him…"*

On Sunday, Katie's mom called to say they would love to have me come over and pray for Katie. Relieved, I set it up for Tuesday after school so Kira could visit Katie. My plan was to come in with Kira, pray for few minutes, and scoot out.

That was my plan. But that's not what happened.

When we arrived, Kira and I sat with Katie and her mom in their living room decorated with cheery photos of birthdays and vacations. As we talked, I had the opportunity to explain how God had been moving in my life. I told them that up until recently, I had not been very spiritual. While I ostensibly believed in God, I was basically just going through the motions, seeking him only when I needed a favor. However, the last few years had been different, I explained. God had truly touched our lives during Kira's struggle with depression, and since then I had felt his presence many times.

I told them that none of my previous experiences were as powerful or profound as when I prayed for Katie. I admitted that my first reaction to God's request was denial, then fear, then embarrassment. I confided I was worried it would all seem too weird to them. The response from Katie's mom was comforting. Since Katie's cancer, she said, nothing seemed weird or strange anymore. They too were trying to understand God in the whole surreal situation.

After talking nearly an hour, I asked Katie if I could pray for her. She got up from the couch, walked over, and faced me. When I looked at the lump on her cheek, I realized it was on her right side. I gulped hard. God had specifically – and prophetically – told me to lay my *left* hand on her cancer. As I remembered his precise words, chills went down my spine and tears stung my eyes. With my left hand on her tumor and my right hand on her shoulder, I prayed for Katie, for her family, for her doctors – and here was the big one – for God to heal her if it was his will.

To this day, I can't remember a word of that prayer. Since I had so little experience praying out loud, I was a little uncomfortable. But even back then, I instinctively knew that God didn't care how I sounded. Without notes or rehearsal, I simply prayed what was on my heart.

When I finished, I opened my eyes to see tears running

down Katie's beautiful face. Her Mom and Kira were also crying. Smiling, Katie gave me a warm hug then skipped off to play with Kira.

As I drove home that evening, I felt an incredible peace about my life. God was using me and I was being obedient. In normal context, "being used" is a negative thing. When we discover somebody's "using us," we feel victimized and hurt. We're angry because we've been set up. But when God uses us for his purpose, there is no more satisfying feeling in the world.

I was also amazed at how easily God arranged the whole situation. What I feared would be a monumental ordeal was effortlessly orchestrated. I was beginning to realize that no matter what he asked me to do, I could totally trust him. That should have been obvious by then, but I was thickheaded and stubborn. Still am. Even today, my lack of trust gets in the way of my relationship with God.

The following week, Gina felt another stirring from God about Katie. From conversations with Katie's mom, she knew there were many incidental expenses that insurance was not covering for the family. She felt prompted to give a gift of money to the family. Without hesitating, she bought a card, put some cash in it, and took it over to the house. Initially she thought about just dropping it off on the porch and leaving. But the moment she approached the landing, the door opened and Katie's mom appeared. Gina stammered out something about feeling prompted to give them a gift and handed her the card.

She looked at Gina and said, "You have no idea what a blessing this is for us. We just spent $500 on a custom wig for Katie but it was the wrong color. The company said they would make another one for $250. We were just trying to figure out if we could afford to buy another one. This will certainly help."

Gina squeezed her hand and walked away with a big

smile on her face. At that moment, only my wife and God knew there was exactly $250 inside the card.

Meanwhile, I hoped and prayed for miraculous results.

A few months later, we got encouraging news: Katie's radiation and chemo treatments were having a positive and pronounced impact in shrinking the tumor. When we called for an update, her mom said the doctors were surprised at how well the tumor was responding to the treatments. Doctors felt it had actually shrunk enough for them to remove it surgically without damaging too many muscles and nerve endings in the facial region. This was the best possible outcome, since removal meant the remaining chemotherapy would only have to impact the residual cancer.

Katie had the three-hour surgery in the fall of 2003. Again, things went amazingly well. While she lost mobility in her jaw and could only drink liquids for several months, initial reports and tests regarding the surgery were very promising. Against big odds, it seemed Katie was winning the fight.

And why not? God had spoken and I had obeyed. As far as I understood the Bible, if I did the praying, he would do the healing. Botta-bing-botta-boom. Everyone says "amen" and lives happily ever after.

Or so I thought.

In early 2004, new MRI scans showed that something in the same region of her jaw was growing back. Initially it was thought to be scar tissue, but by spring the doctors were convinced the tumor was growing again. By late summer, it was clear the growth was very aggressive and Katie began to experience sharp pain. The doctors arranged another surgery, but when she showed up for the final MRI, the scans revealed a discouraging surprise: The fast-growing tumor was now much larger than anyone expected. Worse yet, it had grown into very sensitive areas of her facial nerves and muscles.

The doctors told the heartbroken family there was now only a small chance of success with the surgery. Even if they performed the risky operation, it was highly likely the tumor would grow back again. The odds with chemo and radiation were even worse. When Katie heard the news, she bravely told her parents she did not want to go through with any more treatments. She knew her battle was coming to an end.

The family brought in hospice care to help administer pain medication. I was deeply hurt by Katie's downward spiral. Why would God prompt me to pray for her if he did not plan to heal her? I was totally confused. I knew God had the power to heal. Why wouldn't he use it in this situation?

Faced with the senseless death of a child, I found myself asking the "why" questions to God. Watching Katie suffer month after month stirred up doubts in my heart: *Did I misunderstand God's instructions? Did I do something wrong? Did I even hear his voice to begin with?*

I understood that God's answer to prayer depends on many variables, the greatest being his incomprehensible will. I also knew faith was a big factor in prayer. Once after healing a blind man, Jesus told him *"Your faith has healed you"* (Mathew 9:22). Again, after healing a woman of chronic bleeding, Jesus told her *"Daughter, your faith has healed you"* (Luke 9:48).

From talking to Katie I felt sure her faith was strong. Desperate for answers, I wondered if *my* lack of faith was the problem. When I prayed for Katie, did I really believe God could heal her? I resolved to keep praying for a miracle, no matter how bad things looked. I told God every time I prayed that I truly believed he could heal Katie. Yet I knew that even if my faith was strong enough to move mountains, the outcome could still be different than what I hoped.

In early November, I had another prompting by God to see Katie and pray for her again. Heart racing, I dialed the family, and after making small talk asked if I could visit. A few nights later, Gina, Kira, and I stopped by. Katie was there with her mom and her cousin who had moved in with the family to help out. As we talked, I told Katie that I was still praying for a miracle, but maybe in God's eyes a miracle meant for her to be taken away from this place of suffering and pain.

She looked at me with her beautiful smile and said confidently, "I know that my heavenly Father wants to bring me back home."

She seemed so at peace with this outcome. I was humbled to see the strength of Katie's belief, and it was obvious that her trust in God had strengthened her mom's faith as well. She was truly thankful for the extra time they'd been given with their "precious little angel" as they called her, especially for the summer that had created so many wonderful memories.

Two days after Thanksgiving, Katie took her last painful breath and her spirit flew from this world to an eternity of bliss. Even though I had braced myself, I was devastated by her passing. My family was grief-stricken, especially Kira.

I was out of town when I received the call from my wife. I hung up the phone and went back to asking the "why" questions. No matter how hard I struggled to understand the mystery, I could never solve it. It was a circular thought pattern with no beginning, no end, and no place to find rest or comfort. It shook my faith. It brought back doubts.

All I knew for sure anymore was that I had felt God's prompting to pray for healing and it hadn't worked.

As I walked into the church for her funeral, I was tormented by unanswered questions. My stomach was in knots and my heart was aching. I could not bear to watch the family as they filed in behind the casket. I sobbed so deeply that I had trouble breathing. I have never been through a more difficult funeral. I knew Katie was in a joyous place, but I agonized for her family.

I thought, If I am grieving this hard over Katie, how would I feel if she were my own daughter? As the choir sang praises to God, I clenched my fists and refused to sing. But when the priest spoke about Katie's life, my heart softened. I listened intently to stories of how strong Katie's faith in Christ was. How she comforted those around her. How she urged her family to celebrate her life instead of mourning her death. In her own prayer for her family, she thanked God for her short time here on earth. Her gratefulness to him for the chance to impact her family and friends was overwhelming.

In her last days, Katie did not ask the "why" questions. She simply took it on faith that God's ways were higher than hers. If she could accept her situation as beyond human understanding, why was I so consumed with trying to make sense of it? My narrow definition of victory for little Katie was healing. But maybe God knew better. Maybe if he healed her this time, the cancer would return and cause even more pain and suffering. From that perspective, the alternative – an eternity of peace and joy – sounded much better.

Katie was only 13 years old when she died, but her wisdom surpassed that of most adults. In her death, Katie taught us about life. God used her courage to strengthen my faith and to demonstrate the *"peace of God which transcends all understanding"* (Philippians 4:7).

Because of Katie I realized that God asks us to be obedient regardless of the outcome. In Genesis, he tested Abraham by asking him to sacrifice his son Isaac on an altar. As Abraham obediently raised the knife to kill his only child, God interrupted him: *"Do not lay a hand on the boy… now I know that you fear God… I will surely bless you… because you have obeyed me"* (Genesis 22:12, 17-18).

Following Jesus means following him into the moment – convenient or awkward, comfortable or humiliating, safe or dangerous. It means responding to him whenever he speaks; whether it is about you, your family, or a complete stranger. It's not for us to calculate the outcome of our prayers or actions before we obey. That is in God's control. Our submission and response are all that are necessary. The rest is up to him.

I am convinced that God did not cause Katie's cancer. He doesn't pick out certain people for an experiment so we can learn some grand object lesson about life. That is simply not God's character as revealed to us in Jesus as he walked the earth *"healing every disease and sickness among the people"* (Matthew 4:23).

So if God is so perfect and loving, why such a messed up planet?

We live in a fallen world, an imperfect mockery of the pristine, flawless world God originally created. Unfortunately, sickness and disease are an outgrowth of that imperfection. Adam's disobedience to God brought a curse on the earth and the result of that fall has been pain, suffering, and death for everyone who's ever lived. The good news is that Jesus came to free us from death by taking our punishment on the cross and then rising from the dead to prove his power over the grave.

Whenever Jesus encountered suffering, he was moved with compassion and acted to eliminate it. It's hard to believe, but God loves our children even more than we do as their earthly parents. Surely, he grieved over Katie's suffering and determined what outcome was best. That truth, I simply have to accept.

When I prayed for a miracle according to my understanding of the term, I was disappointed. But surely a miracle *did* happen from God's viewpoint. Only the eternal Creator knows the larger story that has been unfolding for thousands of years. Our brief lives – like dust in the wind according to Solomon – are just a tiny part of this huge redemptive mission God has ordained, and each of us plays a role known only to him.

Without question, Katie fulfilled her role as the heroine in this small corner of God's kingdom. When the enemy tried to separate her from God, she did not waver in her faith. In the end, that's the best any of us can do. On the eve of his torture and crucifixion, even Jesus wrestled with the suffering he knew was coming. But in full obedience to the Father, he said what we all should say: *"May your will be done"* (Matthew 26:42).

I know that many people have been blessed by Katie's story and her life. But I'll never know exactly who or how until the day I join her in heaven. Then and only then will any of us fully see the results of obeying God. And only then will I fully grasp the eternal impact of one teenager's incredible faith on those of us she left behind.

Somehow I'm sure she already knows that full well.

○   ○   ○

"As the heavens are higher than the earth, so are my ways higher than your ways and my thoughts than your thoughts." (Isaiah 55:9)

15

DISCOVERY:
Leaving Jesusland

Sorry, Texas.

But everything really is bigger in the Amazon rain forest. Bigger snakes, taller trees, fatter spiders, you name it. In fact the only thing that's smaller south of the equator is the size of the airports.

The strip of tarmac below us seemed way too short to land on, but after 14 hours of flying, I was ready to kiss the ground. Any ground. Our plane touched down on the stunted landing strip, braked noisily, and taxied to a stop near a rusty metal building. A hand-lettered sign on the side of the terminal read, "Welcome to Iquitos, Peru." By the time we climbed down the stairs to the runway, I swear my shirt was already wet, and the acrid steam of rotting vegetation hit my nose like the mother of all compost.

This was my first mission trip outside the country and I was apprehensive. I was one of ten adult leaders shepherding 40 high school students who had decided to spend their Spring Break passing out the *Book of Hope* to thousands of kids in a remote jungle city at the headwaters of the Amazon River. You won't see *that* on MTV.

An olive-drab bus picked us up at the terminal, and we met some of the locals who would be helping us during the week. The first person I met was Pastor Ramon Sahuarico. I didn't know it then, but this smiling man with weathered skin and deep brown eyes would be my interpreter for the week. Pastor Ramon would accompany my platoon of 12 students into the schools and translate for us during our presentations to the children.

Our plan was to hit 20 schools in 5 days. First, our youth group would break the ice with eye-popping drama skits and mimes, then I would wrap up each assembly with a short Gospel message. Our "street team" consisted of Pastor Ramon, five Peruvian volunteers, and our own energetic high school students.

Our hotel was an aging but impressive stucco building near the main square of the city. When I first heard of the jungle town of Iquitos, I pictured quaint thatched-roof huts in a pristine setting. I was not prepared for the sprawl of small wooden shacks that housed the majority of poor families in this port city of 400,000 residents.

Most areas we visited looked drearily the same, with muddy streets, open sewage, and heaps of garbage. The only exception was near the town square. There, large banks, townhouses, hotels, and restaurants towered above the slums. At each ornate doorway, armed guards reminded me of the huge gap between rich and poor in this frontier outpost.

These colorful European style buildings were remnants of the 1880s rubber boom, and were decorated with ceramic tiles imported from Italy and Portugal. Not far from our hotel stood the famed *Casa de Hierro* (iron house), originally built in Paris by the same Gustav Eiffel who designed the famous tower. The French landmark was purchased by a wealthy rubber baron who had it dismantled, shipped over, and reassembled by native laborers in 1878.

Before the trip, I had envisioned the serenity and peace of the Amazon basin. My first noisy day proved my week in paradise would be anything but quiet. *Motokars* (three-wheel motorcycle rickshaws) are Peru's principle means of public transportation. This fleet of cabs makes a constant racket with unmuffled exhaust, nonstop honking, and plenty of shouting by the drivers. Choking the crowded streets, this strange taxi system is also the largest form of employment in the city. Stick out your hand, and no fewer than five rickshaw operators will race over and fight for your business. Crossing the street on foot means dodging at least ten drivers who seem perfectly happy to run you over. Not surprisingly, these entrepreneurs are up before dawn, cruising the streets for anyone needing a lift.

While traveling for business, my hotel room is usually a tranquil oasis where I have my morning quiet time with God. But in Peru, I was jolted out of bed by the loud buzzing of *motokars* swarming outside my window like angry bees. They were so loud I could barely think, let alone focus on God. To make matters worse, we had to have breakfast as a group and be in the schools by 7 a.m.

I needed to quickly find a sanctuary away from the busy town square, so I left my room and began walking. On the day we arrived I had noticed a street near the hotel that seemed to lead out to open space. Leaving the central hub on foot, I followed *La Boulevard* upward past the cafes, past the street vendors setting up shop, and finally past the city itself until I saw a lush river valley spreading out below me.

By then, the sound of the motorcycles was only a distant hum, and as I reached a stone railing at the crest of a bluff, I saw an incredible sight. As far as the eye could see, the Momon

River bank was dotted with thatched-roof huts suspended on stilts. I stared out into the river valley for a long time as the villagers woke up and began their day. I watched men and women in tattered bathing suits congregate at the only spring in the area to wash themselves. I watched children fetch pails of water to mix with cornmeal for polentas and tortillas. I watched women light cooking fires inside their smoky huts. Everywhere, morning routines unfolded like they had for hundreds, maybe thousands of years.

It was the perfect place to have my quiet time.

I am certain God led me to this place, not only to find the silence and solitude I needed, but to contrast the pampered life I was living back home. Most people returning from mission trips say the greatest life change they experience overseas is an increased awareness of the affluence we take for granted. The second big change is an abrupt shift in priorities – little things that worried them no longer seem so important. Watching the villagers that morning put my suburban life in a whole new perspective.

After observing these destitute people (who God loves as much as me), I sat down on a bench and began to read scripture. I opened my Bible and turned to Philippians. Immediately my eyes were drawn to a single verse, *"I can do everything through him who gives me strength"* (Philippians 4:13).

Did I need strength? Let me count the ways: I was 4,500 miles from home. I was tired from bad sleep and jet lag. I didn't speak a word of Spanish. I didn't recognize the rodent that was served for dinner. I was stressed out by supervising 12 active teenagers in a strange country. Now I was being asked to deliver the Easter morning sermon in the local church my team attended. To make it worse, I had only been informed of this new assignment the night before, and had no time to prepare. If God did not show up, it was going to be the worst

Easter message in South America. If I was going to survive the week, I had to rely on *"him who gives me strength."*

After reading a little more of Philippians, I shifted into my prayer time. I set my Bible and camera down next to me, closed my eyes, and buried my head in my hands. As I prayed, I began to hear footsteps circling the bench. Unknown to me, the villagers were coming up from their huts along the river to begin their workday in the city.

For the first time in Peru, I was afraid.

Was this area safe for foreigners? Did the natives know I was alone? I wanted to open my eyes so badly and look around, but I fought to maintain my focus on Jesus. As I prayed, the footsteps grew louder and closer. Voices were jabbering all around me. Just as I was about to break my concentration and assess the danger, I heard the Holy Spirit whisper, *Trust me. You are in my hands. Center your day on me, and I will give you strength.* That was a lesson I needed – not only for my grueling week in Iquitos, but for my cushy life back home. As the footsteps and murmuring faded away, I pledged to center every day of that week on Jesus.

Later that morning, God answered my prayers by showing up immediately and unmistakably. After jouncing down miles of deeply rutted, unpaved streets, we arrived at our first school. We were all excited to do our presentation, but also a little nervous. When we entered the school, we discovered the principal hadn't arrived yet. The assistant told us to set up our equipment in the back courtyard, and wait for him to come. After some anxious moments trying to find a working electrical outlet, we began hooking up our portable sound system, compact disc player, and microphone.

Dozens of curious children began to fill the courtyard. Then hundreds. By the time we were set up and ready, over 500 school kids had jammed into the small enclosed space.

When the principal arrived, he stormed into the courtyard and immediately went up to Delores, our Book of Hope representative. Fortunately, she spoke fluent Spanish, but I could tell immediately the conversation was not going well. When the brief exchange ended, Delores came over to me, looking discouraged. I asked her what was wrong. She said the principal would not allow us the allotted 30 minutes for our presentation. Instead, he was only going to give us five.

I was floored.

Delores then handed the microphone to the principal and asked if he would like to address his student body. He eagerly took the microphone and began to talk… and talk… and talk.

As he droned on, I imagined how disappointed our U.S. team would be when they found out they could not perform the dramas they had rehearsed for so long. My mind drifted back to the months of practice each teen had put in and the pride they took in memorizing skits tailored for this culture. When I refocused on the courtyard, the principal was still talking. At one point I leaned over to Delores and said, "I don't think he has ever had a microphone before. It sounds like he's running for political office."

Delores chuckled, but I realized I had made an unfair judgment of this man. Immediately, I bowed my head and asked God to forgive me for the comment, and then asked if he would *"soften this man's heart"* so that we could do our full presentation.

As my eyes were closed in prayer, the whole courtyard erupted into laughter. I looked up at Delores and asked what was so funny. She replied, "He told the students that he was originally only going to let us spend five minutes with them, but since he had never used a microphone before, his *heart was softened* and he decided to give us the full time."

I could not believe my ears. It was rare enough to have immediate answer to prayer, but to have another man use my exact words blew me away. On the bus ride to our next school, I debriefed our street team. When I shared the miracle, the kids got totally pumped to hear how God showed up – before we ever hit the stage.

The whole week was full of "God moments." At one campus, there was no courtyard so they asked us to set up in the middle of the street in front of the school. This twist sent us on a frantic search for electrical power. None of the plugs in the school were working. But the principal was so eager to have us perform she even tried to disconnect her electric bell so we could splice into the power line.

After searching for 20 minutes, we were unable to locate power. All of our technology was useless. We decided to perform anyway – without the sound system or music. Standing at the bus, I grabbed a student named Charlie, and asked him to pray with me. The prayer sounded weird because we asked God for power – not his power (we needed that, too) but electrical power. The minute we finished praying, a man living 100 yards down the street walked out of his house with an extension cord and marched straight toward the bus.

He told Delores the power from his house was ours to use.

We plugged in and gave one of the most inspiring performances of the week. In fact, the sound carried so strongly throughout the neighborhood that people poured out of their houses for blocks to see what it was. In the end, well over a thousand men, women, and children heard the message of Jesus that morning. Charlie and I learned that when God wants something accomplished, he will make it happen no matter what.

With each new adventure, I grew more impressed with Pastor Ramon. He was a humble man, and his kind face always had what I call the "Jesus look." I trusted him completely. On our second day, I met a young man named Guido in the lobby of our hotel. I didn't trust him at all. Since visitors from America were rare, he showed up at our hotel and hung around in hope of meeting some *gringos.*

At first glance I thought Guido was just another con artist, trying to sell us more junk jewelry and t-shirts. But as I talked to him, I realized he spoke English well and had a quick mind. He told me he lived in a small village about a 40-minute boat ride away, down the Manicamari River. He said he was a new Christian, and that his father worked in the village church. He went to school in Iquitos and was studying English.

At first, I doubted Guido's story. But as he spoke I sensed he might be telling the truth. Taking a risk, I asked if he would accompany us the next day as one of our translators. I explained that our U.S. students really wanted to talk with the children of Iquitos, but we didn't have enough interpreters. He agreed to come, but said he would need money for transportation to and from town.

My scam detector hit the red zone. Then I sensed God's still, small voice.

Trusting my "holy hunch," I handed him a fat wad of Peruvian *soles* and shook hands. He said he was deeply thankful and disappeared into the crowd.

Next day, Guido showed up, eager to put his skills to work. I breathed a sigh of relief and hugged him. He was an excellent translator and it was great having him with us. Our team really appreciated his help, and everyone was able to directly connect with the students. But on Thursday – our last day to minister in the schools – there was controversy.

It seems the Book of Hope team from Iquitos was jealous of Guido. They were upset that this outsider had not gone through the training to be part of the team. Those who had completed the courses wanted the first chance to travel and work with us.

I told them there was plenty of room for all of them, but what I needed most were more interpreters. When I asked for translators, they admitted that none of the trained team members spoke English. Patiently, I explained that was exactly the reason I needed Guido, and that I wanted him to accompany me.

I asked for grace. What I got was blank stares.

Evidently, protocol was more important to them than effectiveness, and they told Guido he could no longer work with us. I apologized to Guido, then whispered to him to secretly wait for our team bus. When it passed by, he could jump on and join us. I knew I was breaking the rules, but felt this technicality was ridiculous.

As our bus pulled out of the staging area front gate, Guido tried to hop on, but he was pushed off by indignant members of the Iquitos team. I was outraged at this disturbing lack of compassion. I asked the leadership if it made sense to be spreading the love of Jesus throughout the city but denying it to a willing worker just because he lacked credentials. Surely, Guido would wonder why he wasn't shown the same love we proclaimed to strangers. I even worried if rejection by his peers might destroy this young believer's faith.

That afternoon we finished early, and Pastor Ramon asked us if we wanted to visit his church. I was eager to see it, so we coaxed our bus down a muddy two-track as far as it could go. When it bogged down, we exited the bus and followed Pastor Ramon down twisting alleyways until we came to a small unmarked building. We didn't know it then, but we were actually entering his church's back door.

We walked through a catacomb of hallways and small rooms, and then down a long hallway that led to a large chamber. There were about 20 wooden benches on the dirt floor, and the ceiling was tin. Ventilation was a four-foot open air space from the walls to the roof. The pulpit area was like a pitcher's mound of hard-packed earth with a small brick retaining wall. The clandestine atmosphere and makeshift furnishings reminded me of the first-century church meeting in homes and caves to avoid detection.

Pastor Ramon proudly explained they had just purchased this building and worked on it whenever they had the funds and the time. To me, it was the perfect place to worship God, without all of the distractions and comforts of the modern world. While we were visiting, many of the wonderful people from Ramon's congregation stopped by to wish us well. Although it was hot, dark, and dusty, it was easy to see that God was at work in this hallowed ground.

Friday was our last morning in Iquitos, and I wondered if I would ever see Guido again. He had been on my heart during the previous day and night. We boarded the bus for a brief trip to the Amazon River for some sightseeing, but I did not see Guido anywhere. When we returned from our rain forest safari (more touristy than authentic), we packed our bags for the return trip home. As I walked out to the bus for the last time, Guido was there waiting for me.

He had brought a gift for me from his village. It was a straw hat his grandmother had made. I was so touched by his kindness that I broke down and cried. I reached in my pocket for the gift I had brought for him. It was a polished Petoskey stone from northern Michigan. An inscription on this piece of fossilized coral read, "May you build your life on the foundation stone of Jesus."

I had brought several of these stones with me, and handed them out to the young kids I got to know best. But I had saved one last stone for Guido, and prayed I would get the chance to give it to him. I gave him my e-mail address, and said to write if he ever visited one of the Internet cafes in Iquitos. He told me he used the Internet often, and gave me his own e-mail address. I was amazed. Even people living on the Amazon can shop on Amazon.com. I told him I wanted to continue our relationship, and gave him one last bear hug (or anaconda squeeze, if you prefer). As our bus rolled out of Iquitos, I was sad to leave these warm, gentle people who were so precious to God and to me.

Pastor Ramon accompanied us to the airport, and I said my goodbye to him on the runway. He too had an e-mail address, and we promised to write each other. In a week's time, I had become great friends with this man. Why? I believe God knew that once my heart was opened to this man, my wallet would be too. Standing in the tropical sun, I felt led to ask Pastor Ramon what was the one thing his church needed most. Without hesitation, he said they were praying for a sound system. I told him that God had put it on my heart to give a gift to his church. Now it was his turn to cry. I gave him a soggy embrace and waved goodbye as I walked across the hot tarmac to board my flight.

As the plane took off, I wondered if my life would ever be the same. Since setting foot in Peru, my heart had been broken over and over. Jesus had given me a glimpse of the incredible needs in today's world, and I saw how easy it was for us in America to selfishly store up treasures for ourselves.

In the parable of the rich fool, Jesus describes the kind of self-absorbed person I was in danger of becoming: *"And I'll say to myself, 'You have plenty of good things laid up for many years. Take life easy; eat, drink, and be merry.' But God said to him, 'You fool! This very night your life will be demanded from you. Then who will get what you prepared for yourself?' "* (Luke 12:18-20).

I had seen bizarre things in Peru, but the wildest was yet

to come. It happened on Friday night in Lima, the day before we were to fly back to Detroit. We were enjoying ourselves, laughing and joking on a bus ride back to our hotel. The street we were driving on was well lit, heavily traveled, and patrolled by police.

We had stopped for a red light, when suddenly I heard an explosion that sounded like gunfire. I whirled around to see one of our leaders covered in broken glass. Thinking she'd been shot, I dashed to the back of the bus.

What had actually happened was stranger than a drive-by shooting.

The instant we had stopped, a motorcyclist had pulled up next to the bus, smashed out a window, and ripped a backpack away from the arms of Sue Ann, one of our leaders. Before we could react, the thief roared off onto a side street and disappeared. This brazen "smash and grab" robbery terrified everyone. But what made it more horrible was the fact that we had all put our passports in Sue Ann's backpack for safekeeping!

That night, the U.S. embassy in Lima told us we would have to stay the weekend, and have temporary passports issued on Monday. With any luck, we could head home on Tuesday. Maybe. By this time, we were all tired and ready to see our families again. The thought of spending four more days in the congestion and craziness of Lima was not appealing. However, one phone call to my wife put the "Kensington machine" into action. My wife Gina and our friend Nadine made phone calls to church leaders, U.S. Customs, American Airlines, and a local news channel. The Book of Hope people had great connections in Lima, and through a joint effort it looked like we would be able to leave.

The customs agents in Dallas were prepared for us to arrive, and American Airlines was assuring our families back home that they would allow us to board the plane. All well and good. Unfortunately, we had no such assurance from the people in charge in Lima. In fact, the local embassy said do not – under any circumstances – attempt to leave without proper documentation.

We decided to give it a shot anyway.

On the bus to the airport, we prayed and sang worship songs until we arrived. At the airport, a Book of Hope guy named Paul had one of his finest moments. Earlier, he had warned us not to go. A by-the-book type, he tried every way to dissuade us. But as we were heading into the terminal, he had a change of heart and shouted, "Lord, go before us."

And that he did.

The American Airlines agents were more than helpful, and the only tense part was going through customs. Because we had no valid passports or stamped entry visas, the customs agents had every right to prevent us from leaving.

When I entered the customs area, I was supposed to look for a mysterious female agent named Dora. I searched up and down the rows, but every agent had a mustache. Discouraged, I went to the far left booth, and a very manly man examined my visa. Because I had filled it out just moments before at the airport, there was no stamp recording my entrance to the country. He looked perplexed. I looked worried. Visions of legal problems and firing squads filled my thoughts. Just as I was going to ask for a blindfold and a cigarette, the mighty Dora came rushing through the door.

After some heated words with Dora, the frowning agent started to stamp my visa, then hesitated. More words. More veins popping. Again and again he lifted his arm but couldn't bring himself to finish the deed. Finally, Dora pointed her finger at the visa and said something forcefully in Spanish. Reluctantly, he slammed his stamp down on my visa, and then did the same for the rest of the team. With God before us and Dora behind us, we made it out. *No problemo.*

To put the final exclamation mark on the story, the TV news teams in Detroit had heard about our situation, and their reporters met us at the airport. It was amazing to hear high school students sing God's praises throughout every interview. On the 6 p.m. and 11 p.m. news, a half-million Detroiters heard firsthand how God can turn any situation around for our good and his glory: *"And we know that in all things God works for the good of those who love him, who have been called according to his purpose"* (Romans 8:28).

It's been several years since my first trip to Iquitos, and since then I've been back with my family and led other mission teams. I continue to send gifts of money to Pastor Ramon whenever prompted, and our high school small group helped buy his church an overhead projector and a small parcel of land adjacent to his building. As for Guido, God put him on my heart as well, and my wife and I have been paying for his education. His English skills grew more proficient, and today he is in the ministry.

God's "backstage" role in these relationships was revealed in January 2004, when Pastor Ramon traveled to the United States. He came to visit the many friends he made in over 30 years of missionary work in Iquitos. We were honored to have him stay with our family for two days before moving on to his next destination. As always, his face beamed with the light of Jesus. After catching up for a few minutes, he handed me a letter.

It was from Guido.

Puzzled, I asked him how he even knew Guido, outside of the few days he spent with us interpreting. Smiling, he told me Guido was actually his nephew. Turns out Guido lived with his family in the same small village where Pastor Ramon had grown up. His brother was an elder at the village church Ramon had helped launch several years before. While in Peru, I had no idea my two special friends were related, but as always, God was way out front, and I enjoyed the irony.

In the States, much of my faith life was hypothetical. In Peru, it was the real-deal do-or-die kind of faith. In seven short days I learned that God is in control and can be fully trusted. I learned that if a prayer request fits into God's plan, he will answer immediately. I learned that God's love and compassion cross all cultural barriers. I learned that with God's strength, I can do anything. Most importantly, I learned that if I center each day on Jesus, I can get through any situation.

It's humbling to know that the master builder created me to be a partner in accomplishing his will. It's awesome to know he has equipped me to do the specific work I was designed to do even before my birth. And it's awesome to know that God's perfect plan for my imperfect life works equally well in English or Spanish.

○   ○   ○

"For we are God's workmanship, created in Christ Jesus to do good works, which God prepared in advance for us to do." (Ephesians 3:10)

16

SIMPLIFYING:
Walden Pond

If you want to understand what's wrong with Western civilization, look inside today's automobile.

For zero down and low monthly payments, you can enjoy a level of comfort and luxury that Louis XIV could never imagine. I mean, what king ever had a fully-reclining 16-way adjustable throne? What queen ever sat on heated bucket seats with built-in vibrating massage? Today, anyone with decent credit can ride around in a plush cocoon, outfitted with climate control and a ten-speaker stereo. Thanks to easy credit, John Q. Public can select options like onboard navigation, DVD players, and power everything. And to keep mom's soccer team hydrated between matches, one best-selling minivan boasts 15 separate cup holders.

About the only thing the car companies can't offer is contentment.

In Peru, only 1 out of 500 people will ever own a car. Yet despite their poverty, everybody I saw there seemed happy and content. People appeared grateful for whatever they had, whether it was a beat-up bicycle or an ancient motorscooter. Wherever we roamed, we saw folks who were practically destitute laughing, singing, and having fun. Even beggars were quick to smile.

Since returning from Peru, I was haunted by questions: *How could people so poor be so happy? How could anyone be joyful with so few possessions? Even more puzzling, Why did my wealthy friends back in the States seem so unsatisfied?*

Maybe the Chinese philosopher Lao Tzu, knew the answer: "Be content with what you have, rejoice in the way things are. When you realize there is nothing lacking, the whole world belongs to you."

Like Tzu, the apostle Paul understood happiness doesn't depend on material possessions or status symbols. With apologies to actor Ricardo Montabalm, this founder of the Corinthian church obviously didn't need rich Corinthian leather: *"I have learned to be content whatever the circumstances. I know what it is to be in need, and I know what it is to have plenty. I have learned the secret of being content in any and every situation, whether well fed or hungry, whether living in plenty or in want."*

What was Paul's secret? *"I can do all things through him who gives me strength"* (Philippians 4:11-13).

After what I had seen and experienced in South America, the airport reunion with my family was especially emotional. Of course, we were all glad to be back together as a family. But there was something else going on. It was obvious God had done some major work on my heart, and my wife and kids were immediately aware of the change. The obsessive control freak had returned to America seriously humbled. Reeling from culture shock, I was definitely not ready to jump back into the office scene yet. I told my wife I wanted to stay home and process the experience.

She replied, "Well, you probably couldn't go to work

tomorrow anyway." While I was gone, our primary water well had gone bad. To fix it, Gina tried to get a contractor to dig a trench to a second well that fed the guesthouse. No one was available, so my son Chad and a friend had started digging the trench. They were ambitious, but I knew the project was huge.

When I arrived home, it was great to see Chad and his pal Nick tossing out shovelfuls of sandy soil. Amazingly, they had already excavated about half of the 25-foot trench by themselves. Changing into work clothes, the whole family pitched in, and we dug like gophers with shovels, picks, and wheelbarrows. By late afternoon, we were rightfully elated with our progress.

Suddenly, one end of the four-foot-deep trench collapsed.

No one was injured, but we were crushed emotionally. Exhausted, I said, "Let's call it a night. I'll tackle it myself in the morning."

Waking early, I had intended to finish the trench before noon and go into work, but the job took me all day. Turns out, manual labor was exactly what I needed. I was alone with my thoughts, and I could reflect on Peru while digging away. Mostly, I could reflect on what God had been trying to teach me throughout the trip. Over and over, one word kept popping into my head: *simplify*.

God wanted me to simplify my busy life so that I could have more time to experience him like I had in Peru. As outspoken abstract painter Hans Hofmann said, "The ability to simplify means to eliminate the unnecessary so that the necessary may speak."

Over the next several months, God spoke.

During my prayer time, he prompted me to look inward, and I began to see how judgmental and critical I had become over the years. One morning in July, I went out on the deck and randomly opened the Bible. The pages fell open and my finger stabbed a passage in the gospel of Luke, *"Do not judge, and you will not be judged"* (Luke 6:37).

Was this verse an accident or a message from God? I felt sure he wanted me to read that particular passage, but I didn't know why. It bothered me all day, but the lesson really hit home at our church service that Wednesday evening. When Pastor Craig stood up to speak, he said, "Tonight we are going to look at Luke, chapter 6, verse 37."

I nearly fell out of my seat. I looked up to heaven, *Okay, God! I get it. Doesn't take a genius to figure out I have a critical and judgmental nature.*

With God's help, I began to take conscious notice of my harsh comments and unkind observations about people. For weeks on end I worked on areas like sarcasm, inappropriate joking, and judging others. In fact, I was in attitude adjustment boot camp the entire summer. Like a drill sergeant, God was in my face nonstop. As soon as I vanquished one character flaw, he was right there to reveal another. I knew his discipline was for my own good, but there were times I wished he would lighten up or at least say "at ease."

Meanwhile, the word *simplify* was still the recurring theme in my life. I was sure God wanted my wife and I to simplify our lifestyle, but we weren't sure how to go about it. We knew our over-stuffed, over-scheduled life needed streamlining. Somebody once said, "Simplicity is making the journey of life with just enough baggage." In our journey we were lugging enough suitcases to sink the Queen Mary. But how could we trim down to that one perfect carry-on bag?

We talked about downward mobility often, and agreed that simplifying our lives should be a work-in-progress instead of a sudden, drastic change. So, like Bill Murray in *What About Bob?*, we decided to make "baby steps" in that direction. The first thing up for discussion was our country club membership.

We'd been members of a beautiful golf club in southeastern Michigan for nearly 20 years. We had lots of friends there, but since our move to the country, we weren't using it as much.

The issue remained on the back burner until God focused our attention on it with an unusual coincidence. I had just returned from Peru and was coming home from my first day at the office since being abroad. Exhausted, I walked into my house and sat down to sift through a stack of mail. There on top was an innocent-looking envelope from the country club. Inside was an invoice for $2,500. What was this special assessment for? To install mahogany lockers in the men's locker room! When I thought about what Pastor Ramon could do with that money in Peru, it sickened me.

Part of me wanted to remain a member, but I could no longer ignore the contradiction of spending serious money on silly amenities while people were lacking basic resources to live. I remembered the challenging advice of Saint Elizabeth Seaton to "Live simply that others might simply live."

Like a declaration of war, the inner battle to stay or drop our membership was on. Being a member of the club had been a part of my life since my childhood. I honestly couldn't imagine not being there. I agonized over the decision but couldn't let go of this family tradition.

Then one day at lunch, God showed me clearly what he wanted me to do. I was sitting in the outdoor courtyard at my office praying for wisdom about the membership. Suddenly, a verse popped into my head as clearly as any audible voice: *"For whoever wants to save his life will lose it, but whoever loses his life for me will find it"* (Matthew 16:25).

Until that moment, I'd never fully understood what that verse meant. It wasn't that God necessarily wanted me to change my life radically – like selling everything off, or giving up my business to follow him. But whatever distracted me from knowing him in a deeper and more meaningful way had to go. For some, the distraction might be their career or drugs. For others, it might be pornography or gambling. For me, it was my beloved country club membership.

At last, I could see clearly what God was promising. He was offering not just a simpler life, but a better life, one that was really worth living – if I would give up the one thing I clung to so dearly. God was willing to drop a life of love, peace, and joy right into the palm of my hand, but if I didn't release my grip, I couldn't open my hand to receive it.

For the first time, I saw faith defined as a choice: *Give up what you know and what you can see for something you don't know and can't see, with only the promise from God that the life he leads you to will be amazing.*

What a great promise. Because I had taken time to listen to God's voice, I realized the decision to put the club on the chopping block would set me free in a new and radical way.

I stood up, walked into my office, and wrote my letter of resignation to the club. The four-month struggle was over.

The benefits of our decision to leave the club surprised even us. Suddenly, we had a lot more unallocated monthly income to use for God's purpose of touching others for him. As a bonus, our decision sparked our desire to reject the kind of keeping-up-with-the-Joneses consumerism that was pushing our friends and neighbors into debt and beyond.

We saw that no amount of binge shopping can ever bring satisfaction or security. Speaking through the prophet Isaiah (who never had a credit card), God asked his people, *"Why do you spend money for what is not bread, and your wages for what does not satisfy?"* (Isaiah 55:2).

Bombarding us with thousands of messages a day, Hollywood and Madison Avenue seduce us into pursuing an extravagance unknown (and impossible) in 95 percent of the world. Advertisers in the U.S. alone spend over $160 billion a year to make us open our wallets. In the movie *Fight Club*, Brad Pitt's character, Tyler Durden, nailed it: "Advertisements have us chasing cars and clothes, working jobs we hate so we can buy *bleep* we don't need... Our great war is a spiritual war. Our great depression is our lives. We've been raised by television to believe that one day we'll all be millionaires and movie gods and rocks stars – but we won't."

From designer jeans to celebrity fragrances, we're suckered into buying things we don't need to impress people we don't like with money we don't have. From childhood on, we're conditioned to super-size our meals, drive biggie cars, and live in McMansions. Eric Hoffer, longshoreman and philosopher, described this addiction, "You can never get enough of what you don't need to make you happy."

Today, my family is more aware of our responsibility to live open-handedly and share what God has blessed us with. We agree with Gandhi, "Earth provides enough to satisfy every man's need, but not every man's greed."

One of the antidotes for greed is to live simply and eliminate the physical clutter of our lives. As recently as 1960, homes were built with two or three small closets. Today, homes have walk-in closets the size of bedrooms and even the garage can't hold the "stuff" we accumulate like magnets. Cashing in on this glut, the familiar self-storage sites that dot suburbia now rake in over $20 billion a year.

I'm still working on simplifying my personal life, and slowly but surely, we keep responding to the changes God is asking us to make as a family. If you saw our crazy schedule, you'd know we have a long way to go. We spent many years complicating our lives, so we have a lot to undo. Henry David Thoreau's advice rings true, "Simplicity, simplicity, simplicity! Let your affairs be as two or three, and not a hundred or a thousand. Instead of a million count half a dozen, and keep your accounts on your thumbnail."

We're not exactly living in a log cabin at Thoreau's Walden Pond yet. Our suburban life is still frazzled and busy and expensive. But we are making progress sorting out our "wants" from our "needs."

Sometimes (especially when I'm suffering from buyer's remorse), I wonder, *What if my goal in life was not to accumulate as much as I can, but to give away as much as I can?*

What if we didn't cram our possessions into overstuffed closets or lock them up in rented storage, but sold them off or gave them away? What if American author Vernon Howard was right when he said, "Our freedom can be measured by the number of things we can walk away from"?

I was beginning to learn that whether you earn $50 a month driving a cab in Peru or $50,000 a month driving a corporation in America, one principle is true: Giving to others leads to the kind of abundance that material wealth can never provide. It's not an abundance that's measured by the number of cars in your driveway or the size of your bank account, but in the way God himself measures it – by the love you show for those in need.

And *that* is the elusive key to contentment.

○　　○　　○

"But godliness with contentment is great gain. For we brought nothing into the world, and we can take nothing out of it. But if we have food and clothing, we will be content with that. People who want to get rich fall into temptations and a trap and into many foolish and harmful desires…" (1 Timothy 6:6-9)

17

ANGER:
My Own Personal Volcano

I was white collar. He was blue collar. I liked to hunt partridges. He liked to hunt deer. I used a shotgun. He used a bow. I liked to fly fish. He said fly-fishing was for pansies. He thought I was a country club boy. I thought he was a roughneck. He thought I was a snob who only hung out with the beautiful people. I thought he was a jock who only hung out with rednecks.

The deck was stacked against us becoming friends. But real life isn't about personality profiles. It's about forgetting the odds and betting on God.

Even when you'd rather fold 'em than hold 'em.

Dave walked into the *24/7 With Jesus* workshop I was co-teaching in April. I had met him before and knew we both shared a love for hunting and fishing. That was enough for me. Except for a relationship with Jesus, there's no greater bond between men than a love for the outdoors.

I looked forward to having him in my class. But when I looked in his eyes, something was missing. Behind his smile,

Dave looked empty. Drained. Nobody home. Which didn't compute, because from what I heard, he was a committed believer walking with God. Curious, I asked him why he enrolled in the class. He said he had "strayed away from God" over the last year and needed to "reignite the passion." I told him he was in exactly the right place.

Throughout the class, I tried to maintain my focus on the sessions I was teaching, but couldn't get my mind off Dave. The Holy Spirit was revealing to me that he was in pain, and I felt the familiar tug of God on my heart: *Get to know this man better.*

After class, I asked if he would meet me for coffee next Thursday before the session. He agreed, and I wondered what God had in store for me with this new person in my life.

I was unprepared for what happened next.

Before the waitress could bring us a menu, Dave warned me it was going to be difficult if not impossible to restore him to spiritual health. From his menacing tone, I didn't doubt it. If he had ever been in love with Jesus, it was clear he had broken off the relationship. And it had been a rough break-up. Dave recalled for me how he had been the leader of our church's fast-growing men's outdoor ministry. When his brother was involved in a personal tragedy, Dave stepped down temporarily to spend time with his family. During this break, he set up a group to run things in the interim. But to Dave, the transfer of leadership seemed like a hostile coup. He felt betrayed by the men he had trusted. As we drank our coffee, I could see he was bitter about the situation and now hated the same guys who were once his friends.

By our second cup, Dave was practically growling as he spit out the gory details of his "raw deal." He admitted he had totally stopped trusting people and was happiest when no one was around. The longer he spoke, the more I sensed his seething anger. On the job, his co-workers feared him. He always carried a *Guns & Ammo* magazine with him, and it helped perpetuate the image that Dave was a dangerous loner who could lose it someday and shoot up the auto plant. He did nothing to dispel the myth, and in fact encouraged it so people would leave him alone.

I remember looking at him that evening and wondering if anything good or loving was left inside this simmering volcano. He knew every story in the Bible. He could quote piles of scripture. But there was no evidence he intended to apply any of it to his own situation.

Dave's bitterness had hardened his heart. He refused to give his pain over to God and forgive those who had unintentionally (or intentionally) hurt him. At some level, he knew revenge was wrong, that violence would only make matters worse, but he held onto his anger with a death grip.

And it was eating him alive.

Somebody needed to displace this man's hatred with the truth of God's love before he exploded. No doubt this was why God had brought us together, but I was starting to worry about what I had gotten myself into. All I could do was listen, try not to look scared, and try not to judge. I told him I too would be angry over the situation, but that he had to let it go. Putting my game face on, I told him that attending *24/7* would help him restore his relationship with Jesus.

Three weeks later, I met Dave for lunch at a restaurant. I expected to hear positive things about how his life was different after the seminar. Instead, he unloaded a full dumpster of accumulated garbage on me. He was still bitter over the outdoor ministry mess, and he felt that his image in the church had been forever stained.

I pleaded with him to forgive these men and move on. I said his lack of forgiveness – nearly a full year after the incident – was leading him further away from Jesus. I told him to focus on God and not to worry about the opinions of men. I shared scripture and I shared my heart.

Then, just when I thought I was making some headway, Dave threw me the most bizarre curveball yet.

He had long been suspicious that God was punishing him for something. "Now," he said, "the other shoe was about to drop." His wife had recently become pregnant and although it was unplanned, they both felt it was a blessing. Then, midway through the pregnancy, her doctors announced their unborn baby was at high risk for Down's syndrome.

Dave was convinced that God was out to get him.

After having three beautiful girls, Dave surmised that God was finally going to give him his boy, but that he would be handicapped and unable to share in the hunting and fishing experiences he longed to enjoy with a son. He thought a special needs baby would be the tool God was going to use to break him, humble him, and most of all, punish him. He explained that God had used extreme measures in the past to "realign him." I listened intently to his twisted rationale, picked up the check, and walked out more confused than ever.

As I left the restaurant, I wondered if I was the right man for the job. I was not even sure if I liked Dave. While we shared a love for the outdoors, we had very little else in common. Our backgrounds and interests were so different, I wondered if God had confused me with someone else. Surely, I was not the one who was going to reach this man. Even Dave doubted it and bluntly told me, "Many have tried before, but they didn't have the intestinal fortitude to go the distance."

I wanted to back out, but I kept sensing God's love for Dave during my prayer time. Over and over, he encouraged me, *Stay the course. Keep your eyes on the prize.*

Finally, God provided a tangible glimmer of hope in

the form of an unexpected letter from Dave. He was very apologetic for dumping so much "negative crap" on me and wrote, "I tried to warn you about what you were undertaking in the beginning. It would probably be easier to convert 50 Muslims than resuscitate me." But part of him wanted to be healed so desperately that he also penned, "I'm going to help you help me."

With this simple phrase, he was opening the door just a crack to hear what God was saying to him through me.

I responded with a letter to him. I took the gloves off and told him the truth, the whole truth, and nothing but. I told him he was bitter, resentful, ungrateful, unforgiving, and unloving. I said he was not exhibiting the "fruit of the Spirit" that Paul said was the evidence of an obedient life. Dave was a stereotypical macho man, and I was afraid my tough love would not penetrate his proud and sometimes arrogant exterior. At first, he was offended by the letter. Later, he said "the arrow hit true to its mark." Finally, he outright thanked me for my directness. We continued to meet and our friendship grew stronger with each meeting.

Change was taking place in his heart, and he began forgiving those he held in contempt over the years. In September, Dave had a confrontation with his supervisor at work. His boss used almost the exact words I used in my letter to him. Watching God use others in this restoration effort, Dave began to realize just how far he had strayed. A week later, his wife gave birth to a healthy, happy baby boy. God's love and mercy did more to convict and humble Dave than even a special needs baby would have. The night of the birth, he shared how he sobbed tears of conviction, shame, and gratitude in the delivery room. He praised God, exclaiming, "I don't deserve such a blessing! Your love overwhelms me!"

Dave was ecstatic. He felt like his relationship with Jesus

was getting better daily. He was thankful for his little boy and he was reaching out to people again. He invited several of his closest friends over while his wife was in the hospital, and we were up until two in the morning listening to how Dave's heart and life had been changing.

It finally seemed like my assignment was nearing an end. Perhaps now, we could simply focus on our friendship. Dave wanted to get me into bow hunting and I began buying equipment. I went with him to his 40-acre property in the thumb area of Michigan, and we had a blast scouting deer and trading jokes. My counseling and advice to Dave had been effective.

Then one night our roles reversed.

Dave came over to my house to practice shooting our bows. Instead, we mostly talked while he shot. After a string of bullseyes, he leaned his compound bow against a hay bale and asked if I was leading and teaching in the church to win the approval of man or the approval of God. Before I could respond, he challenged me with Galatians 1:10, *"Am I now trying to win the approval of men, or of God?"*

I felt like I had been sucker-punched.

Sputtering, I told him I was pretty sure I was doing it because God wanted me to, but that I would have to pray about it. I took Dave's question seriously, as if God himself had spoken it. After all, Dave too had served in the church and had once been used by God. In the process he had become spiritually proud. He didn't want to see it happen to me, and God was using his life as a lesson. Any relationship that God puts together is never a one-way street. There's always something for both parties to learn, and in this case, it was a warning that I could end up like Dave and walk away from my relationship with Jesus. Next morning, I asked God to reveal my true motives. Like King David, I prayed, *"Search me, O*

God, and know my heart; test me and know my anxious thoughts. See if there is any offensive way in me" (Psalm 139:23).

He responded with four questions that entered my thoughts. I wrote them in my journal: *Am I trying to inspire or impress? Am I trying to encourage others or elevate myself? Am I trying to uplift God or usurp him for my purposes? Is what I am doing for my gain or his glory?*

I knew these questions were from God, because "usurp" wasn't a word I used much, and wasn't even sure what it meant. Despite requiring a dictionary, the questions hit me hard, and I realized that my humility was of utmost importance to God.

It also became clear to me that bow hunting did not fit into my life simplification plan. To be honest, I was mostly doing it to please my new friend, and there was no point in concealing my waning interest. The fact that Dave was okay with my decision to opt out was more proof that our tentative friendship was evolving into genuine brotherhood. Things were looking up. But from what I was hearing in my prayer time, my assignment was far from over: *Stay the course. Your work is not yet finished.*

In fact, the hardest part of all was sneaking up fast.

That fall, Dave got word his shift at the auto plant was being eliminated and he was being switched to working afternoons from 3 to 11 p.m. This was the worst possible timetable. He would be sleeping when his kids woke up in the morning and be gone to work before they came home from school in the afternoon. He felt like he was being exiled from his friends and family. Once again, Dave thought God was trying to teach him something the hard way. He soon fell back into negative thinking, and grew bitter toward God and others. He especially blamed his "lazy bum" co-workers for the demise of his original shift. His outlook went from good to bad overnight.

We continued to meet at our favorite restaurant. One day over a plate of fish and chips, I suggested that Dave might be suffering from depression. Months earlier, he had mentioned his wife thought he was depressed. I didn't think so then, but now I was realizing his negative thinking was chronic. He said he would look into it. I also suggested a book by Erwin McManus called *Uprising*. He said he would get it.

In late December, Dave and I went on a one-day hunting trip on the Au Sable River. It was the last day of grouse season, and we had a great time tramping around the north woods. We saw a beautiful rainbow on the way up (rare for December) and felt it was a good omen. Our conversation was deep and intimate, and I shared my own earlier struggles with control, anxiety, and depression. Until that trip, Dave mistakenly thought I "had it all together" and was grateful for my frankness.

I told him that while my depression had been under control for many years, I recently battled abnormal anxiety and had good results from the same doctor who helped my daughter Kira. I said Dr. Steve was an amazing man who treated me with skill and compassion. My admission of illness piqued Dave's curiosity and he pledged to see our doctor. Somewhere on the snowy trails of northern Michigan, we both realized we had a lot more in common than we initially thought.

The day ended up being incredible, and Dave bagged his first grouse in the late afternoon. While it's always nice to come home with something tasty in your game bag, our greatest reward was knocking down a few more walls of misunderstanding and prejudice. Despite my early misgivings, I had come to love Dave as a brother. He had come to trust me as the same. As we parted, I gave him a copy of *Uprising* and a huge hug goodbye.

Keeping his promise, Dave did see Dr. Steve. After being tested, Dave was amazed to hear that he was "off-the-charts" depressed. He began taking medication for his depression, but did not respond well. Dr. Steve said it would take time to get the dosages right, and that he might feel tired and even a bit more depressed at first. I told him I'd experienced the same reaction from my anxiety medication, and that he just needed to give it more time.

Meanwhile, he was reading *Uprising* with a passion. When I met him again for lunch, the book was highlighted and underlined with notes in the margin. He especially zeroed in on the passages about gratitude, realizing that an ungrateful heart cannot experience healing. In his book, McManus says if we constantly focus on what we *don't* have (self-centered) instead of the blessings we *do* have (God-centered), it's impossible for God to work on us.

After this meeting, I wondered if I had been wrong about something I told Dave early in our relationship – that he did not have to go "all the way back to square one with God." Now, I was beginning to think I was mistaken. Total surrender was exactly what God wanted for him, and I recorded that in my journal.

Despite receiving insights from the book, Dave's depression did not improve. It seemed like the medication was taking longer than normal to have an effect. Worse yet, he was now calling me every day with a barrage of questions. Because of his constant pestering and growing dependence on my help, he began referring to me as Dr. Leo Marvin from the movie *What About Bob?* Problem was, Dave actually started behaving like the neurotic character Bob Wiley. But pest or not, I could see he was in a bad state and needed my "Dr. Leo helpline" to stay open.

Then one day, what had seemed cute and comical turned deadly serious.

Dave called me in a mental state I'd describe as somewhere

below rock bottom. In a low monotone, he said he was not sleeping anymore and was so depressed he couldn't think straight. He no longer felt life was worth living, and wondered if he should just give up and do everyone a favor by taking his life. I knew he had an arsenal of hunting weapons and could easily make good on his threat. Suicide seemed unthinkable because of his beautiful wife and children, but it sure sounded like he might try.

Suddenly, I was in way over my head.

Immediately, I got on the phone with the one man I knew Dave could talk to: my friend and life coach, Lee Gardner. When I described the dangerous situation, Lee called Dr. Steve and the two of them joined forces to get Dave well again. Dave met with Lee the following day. He tried his best to act macho, but Lee saw right through it. In fact, with insight that can only be attributed to God, Lee zeroed in on the heart of Dave's problem – he had spent his entire life seeking approval from men, especially his dad. In his mind, he rarely experienced his *earthly* father's love, so he found it difficult to trust his *heavenly* father's love.

The next night, Dave called to ask if Gina and I would stay after our midweek service to pray for him. He had invited many of his friends, including our senior pastor and one of our elders. That evening, I witnessed a broken man accepting Jesus all over again. With his wife and friends surrounding him, Dave got down on his knees and wept openly like a small child. He cried out to the Lord and asked for healing. We all prayed, and I too wept for Dave. God had finally brought my friend to the place he needed to be – broken and humbled before his maker.

In the beginning, I had figured it was just a matter of getting Dave back on the right path and he would be restored to his former self. But God did not want a restored Dave – he wanted a completely *new* Dave in the image of Jesus. As Dave humbled himself, the Lord lifted him up. From that night on, Dave was a new man, growing a little stronger each day.

God has already used the new Dave in remarkable ways. He has become a powerful witness for the Lord on his job site, a place so tough he used to call it his "proving grounds." Because of his transparency at the auto plant, many workers come to talk with him about their own depression and struggles.

Ironically, Dave has poured back into the man who originally led him to Christ. Although he was a believer, this man didn't attend church, and was private and solitary in his worship. While he did read the Bible, it was not enough to sustain him, and he began to withdraw from God. As Dave put it, he had "only one root in the ground." I'm no expert on horticulture, but a tree can't grow with just one root, and it sure can't bear any fruit. Neither can we. To stay connected with God, we need to nourish ourselves from a deep, wide root system of scripture, prayer, worship, fellowship, service, and (for me) time spent out in nature.

Home Depot may be disappointed, but Dave is no longer "Project Man" – a name I had given him because of the never-ending list of projects he felt driven to complete. In fact, he placed all of his unfinished projects inside a giant wooden crate in his garage, and wrote on the outside, "Not to supercede loving God or loving others." Today, Dave is no longer seeking the approval of man that comes by doing works, but the approval of God that comes by surrendering ourselves.

Dave's story was a lesson in humility for me as well, and I'm thankful that the Lord encouraged me to *stay the course.* I looked inward during this time like never before, and saw things God wanted me to work on in my own life. With each step forward and backward and forward again with Dave, I drew closer to Jesus. In the process, I gained a true brother and came to better understand the necessity of being broken before God. In the words of Dave's kingly namesake, *"The sacrifices of God are a broken spirit; a broken and contrite heart, O God, you will not despise"* (Psalm 51:17).

Through Dave, I learned that "square one" is exactly where God wants us to be – all the time. Surrendering to him is not a onetime event.

It is a daily challenge.

18

TRANSITIONS:
Journey to Womanhood

As I slipped the ring on her finger, Kira looked up into my tear-filled eyes. She trembled in the soft glow of the campfire, and as the purity ring slid down her finger, she began to cry.

With the gold band firmly in place, I said, "By accepting this ring, you are recognizing that God has a perfect plan for you and that if you remain faithful and true to his plan in all areas of your life, and if you remain pure in body, mind, and heart, then God will truly bless your life in incredible ways. Let this ring always be a reminder to you of this day and the pledge you have made to follow God and all of his ways. Let the only ring that replaces this one be one that is put on your finger on your wedding day, by the man that God has chosen for you."

With these words, Kira fell into my arms sobbing, "Thank you, Daddy. This was one of the best days of my life."

I couldn't have agreed more...

○   ○   ○

After the way God showed up in my son's "Journey to Manhood" ceremony, I felt him nudging me to conduct a similar event for my daughter when she turned 13. Earlier in the summer, I had asked my friend Marty if he and his soon-to-be-teenaged daughter Andrea would be interested in a rite of passage ceremony. He was enthusiastic about it, and since Kira and Andrea were best friends, they would especially enjoy sharing it together.

We agreed on a date in September and started making our top-secret plans. Being typical males, the more we talked, the more complicated the event became. When we finally put our pencils down, launching a space shuttle seemed simple by comparison (and a lot cheaper). But being typical males, we were confident we could pull it off.

Earlier that year, I had read *She Calls Me Daddy* by Robert Wolgemuth. When I finished the book, I was convicted to be a more intentional father to my adolescent daughter. I vowed to take her on "dates" that would demonstrate how a proper gentleman treats a lady, and what she should expect from a quality suitor of noble character. I planned to raise the bar so high that no mere mortal would ever measure up to her expectations (Sorry, Kira, I got carried away on that last one).

Almost overnight I took a much bigger interest in her life. And almost overnight I discovered the whole father-daughter bonding thing is trickier than it looks for us men. Conversations and activities with daughters don't come as naturally as with sons, and sometimes I felt like a dancer with two left feet. But bull-in-a-china-shop or not, I was determined to have a stronger relationship with her. Kira already knew I loved her deeply (something I never hesitated to tell her), but I was not spending enough time with her just talking and listening, laughing and hugging. So we began to go on regularly scheduled "daddy-daughter dates" as we called them.

We carved out time, booked them in our day planners, and eagerly looked forward to each date. Sometimes casual, sometimes dressy, we went to movies, dinners, ice shows and plays, but whatever we did, it always felt special, just the two of us. We even had our own secret code when we held hands, something that only the two of us shared. It came straight out of Wolgemuth's book and it went like this:

Four squeezes: *Do you love me?*

Three squeezes: *Yes I do.*

Two squeezes: *How much?*

One big squeeze: *Tons!*

I could always tell when Kira needed a little TLC. She would come up to me and squeeze my hand four times. It was a little thing, but to us it signaled unconditional love and support.

The book also inspired me to conduct the "boyfriend interview" when the time would come. The author shares how he confronted the first boy who wanted to take his 16-year-old daughter out. One Friday evening, a young man named Steven arrived at the Wolgemuth house driving an older sports car he had obviously fixed up. The boy parked the immaculate classic and gave it a loving pat. Opening the door, Mr. Wolgemuth shook hands and asked if he could take Steven's car for a spin.

Steven, taken aback, replied, "No way!"

When the father asked why, the surprised teen blurted out, "I'm not sure I can trust you. I don't know anything about you or how you drive."

Mr. Wolgemuth replied "I'm glad that you feel that way, because that is exactly how I feel about you borrowing my daughter for the evening. Now I want to get to know you a little better before I let you do that."

The pre-date interview that followed was probably more conversational than adversarial, but I'm sure Steven got the point. In the end, he made the cut and was allowed to "borrow" the daughter for the evening.

I thought about Wolgemuth's pre-date exchange and decided that when I find myself in this future situation, I'll add a few extra comments: "Steven, you've been working on your car for two years, but I've been working on my daughter for the last 16, and right now, God has her in pure and original condition. Please return her exactly as you found her."

Then my mind wandered to a less godly place. I imagined that as we sit and make polite conversation, I walk over to my gun cabinet and take out my biggest shotgun. As we speak, I sit on the couch and clean the weapon. Then, when the conversation is ending, I look at Steven right through the huge barrel and ask, "Now you *are* going to return her in the same condition you found her in, right? And you *will* be home by eleven o'clock, not a minute after?"

In my fantasy, Steven is sweating profusely, nodding "yes" like a Bobblehead, and wisely deciding that dating Miss Petherick is too risky.

Despite my over-protective nature (and over-active imagination), the book had a positive impact on my relationship with Kira. While it did not contain a prescription for a "Journey to Womanhood" ceremony, it was the tool God used to prompt me to celebrate Kira's milestone with a ritual that would reinforce her commitment to Jesus Christ and strengthen her for the years ahead.

Finally the day for the September ceremony arrived. Early in the morning, I met Marty at his house and we drove just outside of town to a local campground. We picked out a spot and pitched our tents for the evening festivities. Once we had secured our place for the night, we returned to town, picked up the girls, and drove to a restaurant.

As we left the car, we handed each girl a scrapbook and

a Polaroid camera. Unknown to Kira and Andrea we had planned a *This Is Your Life* moment by planting eight surprise guests inside the restaurant. Each guest was a strong Christian woman who had become a big part of our daughter's lives. Among those waiting for Kira was Nadine (her surrogate big sister), Lisa (her vocal coach), and Heather (a middle school ministry leader Kira adored). The plan was to have lunch and talk about girl stuff – boys, growing up, boys, future plans, and boys. They ate and laughed and talked for hours, but the most moving moment was when each of the mentors read a letter they had written especially for the girls.

Kira said all ten of them cried during the letters. Before leaving, they took pictures of everyone and tucked the treasured letters into their scrapbooks. Marty and I showed up around two o'clock to retrieve them, and we were off to our next mystery stop.

Daughters in tow, we headed to downtown Rochester where we did some window shopping and checked out a sidewalk sale. Then we crossed over to a little tea parlor near Main Street. When we walked in, the girl's grandmothers were there waiting. As Marty and I slipped out to shop for our campfire dinner, the surprised girls and their adoring grandmothers sat and talked. When we returned a few hours later it was an instant replay – the girls yakking about how much fun they had and how emotional the letter readings were.

After the tea party, we headed north toward the campground. On the way, we stopped at yet another restaurant, this time along the beautiful Paint Creek trail. We escorted the girls inside and – surprise – they found their mothers waiting for them at the best table in the place, overlooking the creek on an outdoor terrace. With huge hugs, the girls greeted their moms and the dads took off for one last time.

Co-conspirator Marty and I returned to our campground

to await the arrival of the ladies. We'd bought steaks and other manly goodies for our own meal and we cooked it up over an open fire. It was an awesome dinner, and between bites we enjoyed great conversation. I've found that campfires are great for burning away the civilized facades and disguises we hide behind back in civilization. There, in the rolling hills of Great Oaks County Park, Marty and I let our guard down, and in two hours we learned more about each other than we had in the previous two years.

Just as we were cleaning up the last of the dishes, headlights illuminated our campsite, signaling the arrival of the ladies. We invited them to sit around the campfire, and asked the girls how their day was. They both said it was one of the most magical of their lives. Then my wife Gina and I stood up to read our letters to Kira. Neither of us made it very far before we were overcome with emotion. And why not? Our little girl who had suffered so much was now crying tears of joy, confident and secure in the love of Jesus and the support of her parents.

Marty and his ex-wife Maureen tried to read their letters next, but they too could hardly speak through their tears. It had been an incredible day and an even more incredible night. At the end, we asked both girls to stand and face their fathers. Reciting the words we had composed, Marty and I placed the purity rings on our daughter's fingers. The day-long event was over, and it had left a lasting mark on all of us. The moms drove off and the four of us worked on the girl's scrapbooks until exhaustion set in.

Finally, we crawled into our tents. Reflecting on the day, it was clear to me that God had been with us every step of the way. As crickets lulled the others to sleep, I prayed that Kira would always remember the accumulated wisdom she had heard that day from a dozen godly women and two thoroughly wrung-out dads.

For now, the shotgun plan is on hold. I know that Kira is strong in her faith. We've had many talks about why God feels abstinence is important. She has personally seen the devastation that sex outside of marriage causes. And she knows the sad, grim statistics of her promiscuous PG-13 generation. But most importantly, Kira has heard rave reviews from happy couples who remained pure and heard first-hand how God has wonderfully blessed their marriage and sex life.

Kira and Andrea have made a pact to hold each other accountable, and have both committed to follow God's plan for their lives. They have boldly decided to stand up to peer pressure and risk being ridiculed for not going along with the crowd. They're far from perfect, but when they do occasionally stumble, they get right back up, dust themselves off, and go on trying to be examples of godly living.

As our daughters continue to do life together as best friends, Marty and I see the challenges they face growing tougher each year. As parents, we can never be sure that our children won't make bad decisions despite our best efforts, but we can stack the deck in their favor by laying a firm spiritual foundation. Craig Mayes once told me that bad parenting will almost always lead to bad results. Unfortunately, the opposite is not true – good parenting won't automatically lead to good results. But God gives us solid hope: *"Train a child in the way he should go, and when he is old he will not turn from it"* (Proverbs 22:6).

Often, as in this story, stirrings in the heart are only gentle nudges. It is easy to dismiss these diminutive signs as ambiguous or unimportant. At times I find myself asking God to make it extra clear to me (a billboard on the freeway would be nice) when something is important. But then I realize that *all* of God's stirrings are important to him: *"As the rain and the snow come down from heaven… so is my word that goes out from my mouth:*

It will not return to me empty, but will accomplish what I desire and achieve the purpose for which I sent it" (Isaiah 55:10-11).

What if I had not responded to God's subtle prompting about Kira? How would her life be different without a "Journey to Womanhood" ceremony? Only God knows the answer to that question. All I know is that any prompting from God – however large or small – is a big deal, and it may have momentous implications. When we disregard his call, we miss out on a divine opportunity to experience his love for us.

I wonder how many I have already missed.

19

MENTORING:
Passing The Torch

"Greed captures the evolutionary spirit." So says corporate raider Gordon Gekko in the movie *Wall Street*. This ultimate capitalist, played by Michael Douglas, sums up his version of the American dream: "The point is, ladies and gentlemen, that greed, for lack of a better word, is good. Greed is right. Greed works."

For much of my career as an investor, I lived by Gekko's philosophy. In fact, his self-serving character was a role model for many of us clawing our way up in the financial arena. And while I was busy building *my* personal wealth, a young guy I'd never met was busy building *his* fortune across town. Neither of us could have imagined that later in life we'd cross paths at – of all places – a Christian men's retreat.

It was the first night of the retreat when our senior pastor, Steve, challenged every leader at Kensington to find someone to mentor and coach in the faith walk. He said it was time to start sharing what we'd learned by pouring ourselves into other men; redefining "success" as training our "successors" on a daily basis. As if God was preparing me for Steve's message, I'd heard the same words in my prayer time just a few mornings before. In fact, I came to the retreat not only to restore my own soul, but to bolster some new guys in the process. My friend Craig had been pouring into my life for years, and it was time for me to get intentional about pouring into someone else.

As Steve threw down the gauntlet, I looked around the room to see who God had in mind for me to mentor. Immediately, I spotted a young man named Mitch who I had met earlier when we both worked as volunteers in our high school ministry. A native of Philadelphia, Mitch had come to Michigan to visit his uncle Dan, a former news anchorman who had given up his lucrative TV career to produce videos for Kensington.

Handcuffed (not true) and dragged (partially true) to church by his uncle, Mitch noticed something different about the kids who were "into the Jesus thing." Whatever it was, he liked it but didn't know exactly why. Then Uncle Dan took his nephew south of the border on a short-term mission trip. While in Mexico, the tough kid from Philly realized he had strayed from God and needed to find his way back. Mitch accepted Jesus at an outdoor youth rally and was baptized in the salty waters of the Gulf of Mexico. Feeling the call to serve God, he moved in with his uncle and started attending a Christian college to train for a career in ministry.

It looked like he was the ideal candidate for me.

At lunch, Mitch "coincidentally" sat at my table with five other men, all more than twice his age. His questions and answers were wise beyond his years, and it was great fun to see him challenge the older men in their walk with God. It seemed obvious that God wanted me to invest my time polishing this potential leader.

Or so it seemed.

Despite my friendship and volunteer connection with Mitch, I began sensing that God had someone completely different in mind for me – someone I had never met.

After lunch, we had a two-hour break. To clear my brain, I headed straight for the great outdoors. Walking alone down a trail, I was enjoying one of those quiet conversations with God. Praying softly, I asked him to put the right person smack in the middle of my path at some point during the retreat. I didn't expect such an immediate answer.

Or such a literal one.

Heading to my cabin, I saw a guy walking by himself toward the meeting hall. I said "Hi" as we passed and he returned the greeting. As we continued on in opposite directions, he turned and asked "Hey, aren't you the guy who did that 'Journey to Manhood' talk at a retreat a few years ago?"

I stopped and answered, "Yeah. That was me."

"Well, that was an awesome talk. It really inspired me," he replied.

I stuck out my hand, "Thanks. I'm Jeff."

He grabbed my hand and said, "I'm Dave."

Sizing up this 30-something man, I thought, *What is it with me and Davids?* I knew God loves everyone equally, but I couldn't believe how many Davids he had put in my life. Chuckling at God's sense of humor, I knew at that moment he had set this Dave apart for me to mentor.

We began to talk about the manhood ceremony and how it brought my son and I closer to Jesus. Dave was easy to talk with, and we hit it off well. Tired of standing, I motioned for us to sit down on a huge boulder deposited by an ancient glacier that had inched across Michigan when mastodons roamed the state. We chatted about the retreat, about Kensington, and about Dave's newfound passion for Jesus. Before we knew it, over an hour had passed.

As he shared his testimony, I was reminded over and over of my own life just a few years earlier. In fact, I couldn't believe how much we had in common. Long before I signed up for the retreat (or was even born, for that matter), God knew I would be just the right servant to pour into Dave's life, and he planned our "accidental" meeting to the split-second.

Like me, Dave had started a risky new business on his own. It was in the technology arena and he excelled at working the system. He was a capitalist at heart, and quickly got caught up in the obsession of materialism. He was an entrepreneur, a type-A personality, and a millionaire-wanna-be.

Just like me at his age.

Control, achievement, and self-reliance were the "big three" values for this self-made man. He was a poster boy for the American dream, with all the traits our culture celebrates as attributes of those most-likely-to-succeed.

Unfortunately, the exact same qualities that can open doors to financial success can also be the greatest barriers to following Jesus.

Eventually, the glamour of Dave's financial achievement wore thin. After riding the emotional high of financial power, he began to experience the inevitable let-down fictional broker Gordon Gekko lamented in *Wall Street*: "You see that building? I bought that building ten years ago. My first real estate deal. Sold it two years later, made an $800,000 profit. It was better than sex. At the time I thought that was all the money in the world. Now it's a day's pay."

Like Gekko, money no longer filled the vacuum in Dave's soul.

Thankfully, he and his wife wandered into Kensington in September 2001, and began hearing a message that offered hope and fulfillment. God did not introduce himself to Dave in a brilliant flash of light like Paul on the road to Damascus. Nor did he reveal himself with an audible voice from heaven like Moses on Mount Horeb. Instead, he placed a deep and inexplicable yearning in Dave's heart.

Zipping his hooded sweatshirt against the cool breeze that rustled the pines, Dave explained this spiritual hunger was so strong it sometimes felt like he was sick to his stomach. The aching void made no sense to him. He had a great business, wonderful wife, and beautiful 3-month-old daughter. Life was good, but something was missing.

As Dave sat in the back of the church each week, it was if layers of hardened rock around his heart were slowly but surely melting away. He cried often. He read Scripture. And as he reflected on his "perfect" life, he saw it was a house of cards, a rickety facade built on a foundation of shifting sand.

Like me, Dave had always thought of himself as a good person. After all, he had never robbed a bank or killed anyone. But as God worked on his heart, he started to realize just how selfish and self-centered he was. And like me, he realized that what looked like an ideal life to the neighbors was really a total mess.

When his computer business failed because of 9/11, he went through an emergency reassessment of his life. Fortunately, by then the message of God's love had already penetrated his heart. The man who had tried to run everything by himself realized he had to give up control to Jesus so that he could be formed into a man of character that God could use.

As we shared our stories, it was obvious our spiritual journeys were uncannily similar. Like me, Dave's intellectual curiosity led him to do mountains of research. Like me, he became a voracious reader who needed to understand things in his head before he could believe them in his heart. Like me, he joined a Bible study, and despite being a new Christian started his own men's group.

Jesus was taking over Dave's life in a powerful way, and serious life change was happening.

By the time our paths crossed at the retreat, Dave was firmly convinced that God was real, but thirsty to know more. After the event, we began to meet regularly for lunch. The conversations were revealing and inspirational for both of us. As I encouraged him with solid teaching, he in turn encouraged me with his passionate conviction. I sensed early on that God would use Dave powerfully some day. His life was radically different, and he was already having an impact on those around him.

Now, years later, Dave is a powerful witness. Powerful, but not perfect. He still struggles with spiritual discipline, control issues, and the challenge of living in this goofed-up seductive world as a follower of Jesus. These temptations are *"common to man,"* and God knows this (1 Corinthians 10:13). That's why there are no "Lone Rangers" in his kingdom. We are to encourage and exhort one another weekly, daily, hour by hour if necessary.

But what if our schedule is already maxed out?

The apostle Paul was a pretty busy guy. Evangelizing the known world, writing two-thirds of the New Testament, and starting churches kept him tied up (literally and figuratively). But between shipwrecks and beatings, he still found time to pour into a young disciple named Timothy. Paul's priority set the example of how we are to strengthen others in their faith – mentoring and guiding them in their journey of coming to know God more fully.

I've often heard our life in Christ compared to a long-distance marathon. In fact, the Apostle Paul urges us to *"run with perseverance the race marked out for us"* (Hebrews 12:1).

But personally, I think it's more of a relay race. Like a

runner in a relay, we are to "pass the baton" of our knowledge to the next fresh runner who then passes it to the next and so on.

But how do we find our "Timothy"?

We don't.

God does.

I'm convinced if we spend time in prayer, God will reveal who he's selected for us to pour into. And if we haven't actually met this person yet, he'll even arrange the rendezvous.

So suck it up and stick your neck out. Ask God to bring someone across your path who will be a reliable and trustworthy pupil; someone you can instruct so they can teach others about the amazing love and power of Jesus.

And get ready to pass the baton.

○   ○   ○

"And the things you have also heard me say in the presence of many witnesses entrust to reliable men who will also be qualified to teach others." (2 Timothy 2:2)

20

COMBAT:
A Million Gods

Doubting Thomas got a bad rap. Sure, he was a little slow to catch on, but when he did, there was no stopping him.

Here's what I mean: When Thomas demanded proof of the resurrection, Jesus invited him to put his fingers in the holes in his hands. The instant Thomas saw the scars with his own eyes, he declared *"My Lord and my God"* and never looked back.

Doubting Thomas did not stay a doubter.

Church history tells us Thomas fulfilled the Great Commission by transporting the gospel to ancient Babylon (today's Iraq) and then to Persia (today's Iran). Later, in A.D. 52, he sailed south to the west coast of India. Preaching relentlessly, he established churches and converted even the high caste Hindus of the region. Finally, Thomas traveled to the east coast of India, risking his life to evangelize the area. Known as the Apostle of India, he was martyred in A.D. 72, near the present-day city of Madras. While declaring Jesus to the Hindus, he was thrown into a pit and impaled on a spear by a Brahmin priest.

So enough with the nickname, already.

When Portuguese explorers landed in India in the early 1600s, they were amazed to find a group of Christians worshipping at the *Mar Thoma* (Saint Thomas) Church established by old Tom himself a millennium and a half earlier. Thanks to him, Christianity came to India long before it went to England or Western Europe. Unfortunately, it failed to flourish. After 2,000 years of evangelism, only 2 percent of India's population is Christian.

Tough crowd.

Tough and big. Big as in 1.3 billion people big. India's already the second largest nation on earth and will soon pass China. The population of India is equal to all the people in North America, South America, and Africa combined. The cities of Calcutta and Mumbai (formerly Bombay), each have 10 million people. Parts of Mumbai are so densely populated that over 1 million residents are jammed into each square-mile.

India is a study in contrasts. They are nationalistic, but speak 15 official languages. They have nuclear technology, but 390 million people beg for a living. They profess tolerance, but violence against Christianity is growing. 85 percent are Hindus. 10 percent are Muslim. The odds against making an impact for Jesus in such a place are awesome. But so is the faith of a modern day Thomas named Jaya Sankar…

o   o   o

Jaya grew up in a high caste Hindu family. Like all Hindus, his father and grandfather taught him from birth that there were thousands of gods who looked after them. But around the age of 12, Jaya began to question his Hindu beliefs. Things he had taken for granted began to puzzle him, like why hungry people sacrificed valuable food to a myriad of gods.

Every spring, the families in Jaya's village celebrated a holiday called the "festival of the gods." Each family would prepare a sumptuous feast and set out the very best foods on a long, narrow table about a foot off the ground. Then each family would leave their home and invite the gods to come in and partake of the offering. When they returned and saw the food gone they assumed the gods had come for their annual meal. But even as a young boy, Jaya doubted the gods were responsible. Like Thomas, he had to see to it to believe it. So one year, he hid himself in the closet of his home when everyone left. Silently, he stared through a crack in the door and waited for the gods to appear. After two hours, he heard a stirring. Could this be the gods? Standing on his tiptoes to see the spiritual beings, the shocked boy saw a swarm of rats invade the home and devour the food.

When his family returned that evening looking for Jaya, he confronted his grandfather with his discovery. In a rage, the old man beat him and told him the gods could take on any form, including rats. In fact, he said if the gods weren't gracious enough to appear as rodents, anyone beholding them would be blinded by their glory. The brutal beating kept Jaya in line for a while, but his doubts continued to grow.

One day he discovered an old trunk belonging to his grandfather. Inside, Jaya uncovered ancient papaya leaf manuscripts of the Hindu *Vedas*. Burning with curiosity, Jaya pored over the crumbling documents. He read in the *Vedas* that sacrifice was necessary to know God, but that it could not be the sacrifice of an ordinary man born to a sinful father. It had to be the sacrifice of God himself in the form of man, dying to shed his blood for the remission of sins.

Jaya was certain that none of the gods he or his family worshipped fulfilled this mysterious prophecy.

He also came across a description of a god called the

"god of light." When he asked his Hindu priest about this god, the religious leader pled ignorance. However he did say there was a holy man in a nearby village that knew all about the god of light. Intrigued, Jaya walked off to see this man. Sitting cross-legged on a stack of pillows, the bearded mystic said that if Jaya wanted to see the god of light, he would have to immerse himself in the Krishna River each night for 100 consecutive evenings and chant a special prayer 100,000 times. If he did all of this perfectly, the priest said, then the god of light would appear.

The priest appeared confident about the deific appearance, perhaps because he was certain no one would ever perform the mind-boggling requirvements. But Jaya was a very determined young man, and for 100 nights, he stood up to his waist in the cold, filthy river and chanted. Shivering, he prayed out loud as dead animals and human excrement swirled by. As weeks wore on, his skin shriveled and he grew sickly. Each night, leeches sucked his blood and boils broke out from the fetid water. Finally, after three months of chanting, he reached prayer number 99,999. As he nervously spoke the final, magical chant, Jaya looked in all directions and waited for the god of light to appear.

Sadly, the only light was the moon's reflection off the river in the midnight darkness.

Jaya was distraught. He wondered if he had done something wrong or missed a chant. He was certain he had followed the rules exactly. When he questioned the local priest, the old man was equally puzzled. But he did suggest Jaya visit the high priest who lived 300 miles away. Although he was only 14, Jaya began to make plans to see this guru. The local priest arranged for a chaperone to help Jaya on the journey. Since he could not tell his family, he would have to run away secretly and return to face the consequences.

With the priest's assistant helping him, Jaya boarded the train for his second quest. Halfway there however, the not-so-holy holy man disappeared with all of Jaya's belongings, including his money.

Exhausted and nearly starving, he returned to the Rajamundry railway station. He was devastated by this double-cross, particularly since he was supposedly in the care of a godly adult. Too ashamed to return home, he sat down on platform and sobbed. As he stared down the long dark tracks, the steel rails narrowed and met in the distance. Alone and dejected, he decided to put an end to his misery.

In the stillness, Jaya heard the faint rumble of an approaching train. He lay down across the railroad tracks, and began to pray. His request was simple, "God of light, if you are real, reveal yourself to me now for I am about to take my life." Then he heard the most unbelievable words he had ever heard. An audible voice proclaimed, *Jaya, I am the God you are seeking. I am the God of Light. My name is Jesus.*

By this time, the speeding train was only seconds away from crushing him. Then, as Jaya looked in the direction of the voice, he saw a vision of a man he now believes was Jesus Christ. He doesn't remember exactly what happened next, but he felt the train rushing by with the fury of the wind and a noise that drowned out everything around him.

And he was alive.

Standing up beside the steel rails, he declared, "Jesus is the God I have been seeking." He knew then that he had a reason to live and a purpose to fulfill.

When Jaya returned to his village, his family was overjoyed that he was safe. No one had known where he was or why he was missing. After a tearful reunion, Jaya told his family what had happened on the railroad tracks. He told them about trying to kill himself and how Jesus, the God of Light, had saved him. Upon hearing the name "Jesus," Jaya's grandfather flew into a violent rage. He beat the boy severely and forbid him to ever mention the despised God of the Western cultures.

But there was another reason Jaya's grandfather was angry. In India, each level of society adopts a different group of favorite gods, proudly displaying the idols on their mantle and praying to them for favor and protection. Many of the lower caste – beggars, lepers, and other "untouchables" – believe Jesus is one god (little "g") among millions of others, and look to him for help. Consequently, the wealthier Hindus look down upon the poor and their "god" Jesus as scum.

It would be a long time before Jaya actually gave his life to God.

When Jaya finished his formal education, he had mostly forgotten his experience with Jesus. His goal was to "start a vast business and become a rich man in the world." However, while traveling on a motorbike, he had an accident that fractured his right leg. He was treated in the hospital, but after two months the leg had not healed. The pain was unbearable. He could barely walk. When he returned to the hospital, doctors said that unless the leg improved, they would have to amputate.

In India, amputating a limb is like conferring a death sentence because handicapped people are considered untouchables. Alone in the empty hospital ward, Jaya once again felt like ending his life. Then he remembered what Jesus had done for him on the tracks. Lying on his back in the stifling heat, Jaya prayed to Jesus, asking for forgiveness and help. He vowed that if he were healed, he would dedicate his life to ministry.

Soaked in sweat, he felt drowsy. Drifting in and out of consciousness, he heard a sweet melodious voice and felt someone touching his leg. When he awoke moments later, the pain was gone. When the doctors returned, Jaya asked who had been in his room singing and massaging his twisted leg. They replied "no one." He asked what they had done to relieve his agony. They replied "nothing." Two days later, Jaya was up and walking, his leg totally and unexplainably healed.

Shortly after that, Jaya sensed God speaking a verse to him. He located a Bible and searched until he found the passage. It was Romans 9:17, *"I raised you up for this very purpose, that I might display my power in you and that my name might be proclaimed in all the earth."*

After this series of miracles, Jaya committed his life to full-time ministry in 1986. He opened a small church in his home in Dowlaiswarum, a village outside of Rajamundry, a larger town in India's southeastern region. In those early years, he met with great resistance from his community, and was expelled from his own family.

After five years of estrangement, his family contacted him to say his father was stricken with cancer. By the time Jaya was informed of the illness, his father was virtually a living skeleton. Doctors gave him only a few short days to live. Under these grim circumstances, Jaya and his wife were invited inside the family home to say their final farewell. Standing beside his father's deathbed, they prayed boldly for a miracle that would reveal God's power. To the doctor's amazement, his father's frail body was completely healed.

And so was Jaya's relationship with his family.

One by one, his father, mother, brother, and sister committed their lives to Jesus. Soon, other villagers who had been Hindus for a hundred generations began turning away from worshipping idols and false gods to discover the reality of Jesus.

In June of 2000, Jaya made a trip to America to visit a church and foundation in Chicago that were his sole U.S.

supporters. During his stay, he "coincidentally" met the nephew of Kensington's senior pastor, Steve Andrews. Steve's nephew suggested Jaya call to arrange a meeting. He did, and Steve invited Jaya to meet the Kensington team. It was at that meeting Jaya first shared his phenomenal story. Steve and my friend Craig Mayes recognized God's hand on Jaya's life and pledged to visit him in India the following December.

On their first trip to India, Steve and Craig traveled 39 hours to reach Jaya's ministry in remote Andhra Pradesh. There, surrounded by poverty and suffering, they listened to the ambitious dreams Jaya felt were inspired by God. They saw the need was great. They saw the resources were limited. But they also saw that with virtually no budget, Jaya had already accomplished amazing things. Right before their eyes, Jaya was living out one of Steve's favorite scriptures: *"Religion that God our Father accepts as pure and faultless is this: to look after orphans and widows in their distress and to keep oneself from being polluted by the world"* (James 1:27).

One blistering hot day, Jaya took Steve and Craig to a vacant parcel of land near his house. Jaya felt strongly that God had given him a vision for this land to build a campus that would minister to the poor, the orphans, and the widows of India. Joining hands, Steve and Craig prayed with Jaya over the land. They knew the likelihood of anyone – let alone a penniless pastor – being able to obtain such a large piece of property in the heart of his community were slim.

When Steve and Craig returned from India and told our congregation about Jaya's needs, Kensington was in the midst of a capital campaign to raise money for a much needed training center and chapel. But God was already moving behind the scenes to answer Jaya's prayers. Before one dollar was raised, Kensington's leadership had decided that 15 percent of whatever came in would be given away to help other churches outside of Kensington.

Miraculously, the "MaxImpact" fundraiser was a huge success with over $13 million pledged. Thanks to people in Michigan taking a financial risk to obey God, Kensington now had a budget to plant new churches around the world – including India. That day, Jaya received an encouraging long-distance call: Kensington would buy the land and help build his ministry campus.

In January 2003, Jaya made another trip to the United States to visit Kensington regarding ongoing support. By this time, I was meeting with Craig regularly, and he asked if my family would take Jaya out to dinner because he had another engagement. Gina was busy, but I thought it would be great for our kids, Chad and Kira, to meet Jaya. At a restaurant near our house, we peppered Jaya with dozens of questions, trying to understand what life in India was like. He always had the same answer: "You must come and see for yourselves."

At that exact moment I knew I would be going to India. I wasn't sure when, or how, or if my family would come along, but I felt God pulling on my heart to see the work Jaya was doing first hand.

It didn't take long.

Leaving Detroit on a wintry day in February 2004, I fastened my seatbelt for the first leg of a 20-hour flight to India with Craig Mayes and a missions team of 14 people. Craig brought his daughter Megan, and I took Kira. After months of preparation, I was excited about my inaugural journey to Asia, despite the grueling travel ahead of us.

As Craig and I readied our teaching materials, one dark cloud hung over the trip. Six months earlier, an organization involved in India warned our leadership that Western churches like Kensington often had bad experiences in India. We were told to be suspicious of Jaya and to check out his background thoroughly. They even made some unsubstantiated allegations regarding Jaya and his family.

Craig and I suspected ulterior motives behind the warnings. We knew that many Christian organizations in India did not cooperate with each other and were jealous when other groups received financial support. Craig asked me to assist him in sorting out the allegations face to face. On the plane to Mumbai, we agreed to set aside time to talk privately with Jaya.

After traveling 9,615 miles on three planes, one train, and a rickety bus, we finally arrived in Dowlaiswarum. Pulling up in a cloud of dust, Craig was amazed to see the complex of buildings now standing on what had been just a barren plot of land. A large gate with the words "Christ's Evangelical Mission" guarded the campus entrance. Behind it stood two four-story buildings with classrooms and safe housing for the orphans, a sewing school for the widows, and office space for the ministry. Two open-air, thatched roof buildings housed an English school and the Missionary Training School. There was also a small medical clinic that treated local residents. In just a few short years, the land that Craig and Steve had prayed over was totally transformed.

Across two continents, God was doing extraordinary things through ordinary people who simply listened and obeyed his voice.

Once classes were in session and our free medical clinic was underway, Craig and I were able to break free to sit down with Jaya. We talked through all of the issues and concerns raised six months earlier. Jaya was heartbroken and troubled over the suspicions. He was certain the attacks on his character were spiritual warfare. Speaking softly, he offered explanations and answered our concerns. As he spoke, it was clear to me that this man possessed an incredible servant's heart, totally dedicated to spreading the love of Jesus.

In my business, I have met with hundreds of CEOs, politicians, and famous people, but I had never been in the presence of a greater man than Jaya. As he opened his heart to us, I heard the distinct voice of God say, *This man who sits before you is a great man. With him, I am well pleased.*

Overcome by emotion, I shivered as chills ran up and down my spine. I knew going into the meeting that I needed to remain objective and analytical. Objectivity is necessary in my business. But every time God moves in me, it triggers overwhelming emotion. Once again, I knew beyond a doubt that I was hearing God's voice.

After the meeting, I couldn't discuss Jaya without tears welling up. Same for Craig. We both felt Jaya's godly response to the harsh local opposition was evidence that God would continue to do amazing things through him.

The rest of the week was a whirlwind. Our medical team treated over 2,000 patients in a four-day period. Dr. Sal, the Kensington dentist, pulled nearly 200 infected teeth. Even Craig and I got into the action and yanked a tooth or two. Dr. Brad, the Kensington surgeon, saw hundreds of patients, and performed lumpectomies in the open-air clinic. Removing the disfiguring growths not only eliminated the pain but the stigma and discrimination that went along with them.

Meanwhile, my daughter Kira worked in the English school, teaching Indian children new songs and games that improved their language skills. She said her biggest take-away from the trip was contentment – the simple (but profound) realization that she had everything she needed. She also pledged to stop thinking of me as her personal ATM machine. Sadly, that revelation only lasted a few weeks before I was back to dispensing cash at the pre-India rate. Despite my flatter wallet, I knew the seeds planted during this trip would germinate in Kira's life for years to come.

The work was backbreaking, the hours were long, and we all missed air conditioning. But there were humorous moments as well. One day, Craig put me on the back of a motorcycle to show me the Godivari River. After dodging pedestrians, bicycles, ox-drawn carts, people-drawn carts, trucks, buses, and the occasional sacred cow, we made it to the road that led to the river. Zooming along, we narrowly missed several water buffaloes walking in the opposite direction. Even at 30 miles-per-hour, I couldn't help but notice their dangerous-looking horns. I wondered out loud to Craig why these huge animals didn't gore people as they roamed freely through town.

When we arrived at the river, there was a lone water buffalo standing in the middle of the street. I jumped off the motorcycle with my video camera and stopped about five feet in front of this seemingly docile creature. Thoughts of seeing my close-up footage on the Nature Channel went through my mind. As I looked through the viewfinder, I noticed the animal lower his head. I assumed he was reaching down to eat something, but when his head stayed down, I realized he was preparing to charge. Suddenly, the 2,000-pound buffalo came at me like a bull attacking a red cape.

Unfortunately for *America's Funniest Home Videos*, I accidentally hit the stop button or I might have captured the chaos that ensued. I turned and ran away from the river with the buffalo locked in hot pursuit. He only abandoned the chase when I ducked behind the motorcycle, wheezing and out of breath. All the while, the local Indians were laughing wildly at the spectacle. Craig joined the chorus, kindly noting, "The reason the residents don't get trampled or gored is because they're too smart to stand in front of a one-ton buffalo and wave a shiny object!"

Another funny incident happened after our Sunday

service. Each morning the orphans and students walked over to the church on the second floor of Jaya's four-story building. We always attended the worship ceremonies and Craig usually delivered a short message. On this day, Craig taught the story of Jesus feeding the 5,000. He boldly told the kids that whenever they faced an impossible situation they should not worry, but simply remember how Jesus multiplied five loaves and two fish to feed the multitudes. In conclusion, he urged them to never forget the "Lesson of the Loaves."

Twenty minutes later, Craig and I were sitting in Jaya's living room, discussing how we could buy beds for the orphans who were sleeping on mats on the floor. Craig had received a $10,000 donation before the trip and figured we could buy enough beds for everyone with the money. But Jaya reminded us that 40 missionary students did not have beds either, and 30 more orphans were scheduled to arrive in May. To accommodate everyone, Jaya said he needed 100 beds. In my head, I quickly calculated the financial need was $30,000, or three times the amount we had. When I glanced over at Craig, I saw a pained look on his face.

Discouraged, Craig sadly told Jaya, "I just don't know how we could possibly come up with money like that," but as he apologized, he was interrupted by my outburst of laughter.

"Craig," I chided, "remember your famous 'Lesson of the Loaves'?"

I didn't have to say another word. My friend with the big faith and the short memory started laughing out loud, and the irony of his doubts provided comic relief for the rest of the week.

My India experience convinced me that spiritual warfare is very real, and leaders like Jaya have a huge target painted on their back. The more powerful and effective someone is for the Kingdom, the stronger the enemy's attacks against him will be. Thankfully, God is all-powerful and will even work through ordinary people like you and me to overcome the unseen forces of evil.

Jaya's work continues to grow and I have no doubt his immense vision to reach a million souls by the year 2010 will be achieved. As of this writing, his ministry has planted 80 new churches, trained 500 new pastors, and reached 70,000 children at camps and crusades. He's distributed 3 million Gospel tracts, given out 50,000 Bibles, and provided free health care to over 100,000 people. He operates a school, a hospital, an orphanage, and a vocational training center.

All on two meals a day and six hours of sleep a night.

Business author Sandra Swinney says, "It's amazing how much people can get done when it doesn't matter who gets the credit." Because Jaya is willing to give God all the credit, amazing things are happening on a daily basis through the obedience of this soft-spoken man.

○   ○   ○

"Let him who boasts boast in the Lord. For it is not the one who commends himself who is approved, but the one whom the Lord commends." (2 Corinthians 10:17-18)

21

FORGIVENESS:
Selective Amnesia

Every 12 months, the swallows return to Capistrano. Every 12 months, the Monarch butterflies return to Pismo Beach. And every 12 months, flabby Americans return to the health club.

Unfortunately, my annual fitness plan starts with good intentions, then ends with procrastination, excuses, and a major bowl of Hagen Daaz.

But I'm not the only one who fizzles out. Statistics say 99 percent of all New Year's resolutions are broken within one week. And no wonder. People inevitably resolve to do things that are nearly impossible. Blame it on the champagne or wishful thinking, but experts say the most common yearly resolutions are also the toughest: lose weight, save money, stop smoking, start exercising, quit drinking, get out of debt, and learn a language. *Whew!*

Nothing on that list is what I'd call easy. Which explains why obesity is still an epidemic, personal savings are at an all-time low, and millions of treadmills wind up as high-priced clothing racks (I suggest buying a model with padded handrails that won't wrinkle your pants).

But as tough as these classic resolutions are, they're easy compared to saying "I forgive you" to someone who's hurt you.

Especially if that someone is next of kin…

○   ○   ○

I first met my future wife Gina in high school. And although I was genuinely crazy about her, she was insecure about herself and distrustful of others. Including me. When I told her I loved her she refused to believe me.

Even as we grew closer, she was always worried I would walk out on her. She said she was afraid to lower her defenses because she couldn't bear the thought of being hurt again. Things she had loved before had been taken away, and it was an ordeal she couldn't repeat.

I didn't understand her reluctance until she gave me a glimpse into the painful world of her childhood.

When Gina was 7 years old, a drunk driver ran a red light and killed her mother, Eva, in a grinding crash. In an effort to console her, well-meaning adults told her that God must have needed her mother in heaven. Gina never understood that macabre explanation. Lying awake at night, she wondered how God could possibly need her mom more than she did as a young girl. It made her angry to think God snatched her mother away. Confused and bitter, Gina did not develop a positive relationship with God until much later in life.

Soon after the accident, Gina's father Tony started dating Sandra, an attractive woman a dozen years younger than himself. Within a year of Eva's death, Sandra and Tony were married. When I met Gina seven years later, Sandra and her father were getting divorced. The years in between those events had been a living hell for Gina. Through her tears, Gina told me how Sandra abused her mentally and physically.

From one day to the next, she never knew which Sandra would show up – the sweet lady or the wicked stepmother. Gina was verbally degraded and told she would never amount to anything. Her birthdays were barely acknowledged. Once she was kicked and stomped with high heel boots as punishment for raking the shag carpet the wrong way. This violent attack left her legs covered with bruises and open cuts.

Unfortunately, her busy father was oblivious to what was happening – until the day Gina's brother, Jim, caught Sandra in the act.

Jim walked in from school one day to find Sandra beating Gina in the kitchen. He rushed over to Sandra, grabbed her by the throat, and lifted her up against the wall. As her legs dangled above the kitchen tile, Jim warned her, "If you ever touch my sister again, I will kill you."

When Jim told their father what had been going on, he was shocked and sickened. Tony immediately confronted Sandra, but she denied the charges. The grief-stricken father knew his children were not lying. He also knew Sandra had been using drugs and was not mentally stable.

Finally, he and the kids confronted Sandra about the abuse. She flipped out and started screaming and throwing things. Gina, Jim, and their father ran for the door to escape a barrage of flying objects. As they fled, Sandra picked up a steel claw hammer and hurled it across the room with deadly force. It impaled itself into the closet door just inches from Tony's head. Shortly after this outburst, Gina's dad filed for divorce to close a horrible chapter in Gina's life.

Her nightmare seemed over.

Several times during the separation, Sandra enlisted the help of her sympathetic brother to break into Gina's house to take things from the family she thought were hers. Gina noticed something very strange about the break-ins. Every time Sandra entered the house illegally, Gina's watch would mysteriously stop. At first she thought it was just a bizarre coincidence, but after two or three more times, she felt that maybe her deceased mother or God was warning her. A week later she was sitting in algebra class when she glanced down at her wrist. For no apparent reason, her watched had stopped. She immediately called her father. He rushed home to find that Sandra had indeed broken into the house again and robbed it. Unfortunately, this time she took the most precious (and ironic) reminder Gina had of her former life – her mother's watch.

When I met Gina, she was in the middle of all this turmoil. Twice, Gina and I went to Sandra's house to ask for the gold watch back, but her 250-pound bodyguard brother blocked us from coming in to talk. He even threatened us with physical harm if we ever came back. At a strapping 135 pounds, I took this warning seriously. Protected by this bully, Sandra screamed at Gina to get out of her life and taunted that she would never get her mother's watch back. Gina was hysterical and in tears. She could not imagine what she had ever done to deserve such torment.

For me it was like watching a bad horror movie, but at least I finally began to understand the root of Gina's insecurities. Despite the frustration, we both felt that somehow God was looking out for Gina, and that we had been brought together for a new and happier chapter. Today, after celebrating 21 years of marriage, I can honestly say she is much stronger than me, and I marvel at how well she turned out despite overwhelming odds.

As months turned into years, Gina outgrew the feelings of hatred toward her stepmother. And although they never spoke to each other, Gina forgave Sandra in her heart for the abuse she had suffered: *"Be kind and compassionate to one another, forgiving each other, just as in Christ God forgave you"* (Ephesians 4:32).

Gina had completely moved on with her life, and her rotten childhood actually inspired her to be an outstanding mother. She made sure birthdays and holidays were always extra special. She told our kids "I love you" more times in one day than she had heard in seven years from Sandra. As a loving, nurturing mother, she worked hard to erase the memory of her tormentor.

She also worked hard to make sure that for 23 years she and Sandra never *ever* crossed paths.

Then one day in February 2004, Gina drove into our old community and passed by Sandra's home. She had driven past the house hundreds of times before, but had never once seen her stepmother. She even wondered if she still lived there. On this particular day, though, Gina was "meant to" see Sandra standing on her front lawn. She couldn't believe her eyes, and the accidental sighting caused painful memories to resurface. Gina drove on into town to take care of some shopping, then stopped by her father's hair salon to tell him about seeing Sandra.

When Gina walked into the salon, Tony caught her reflection in the mirror. Turning to face her, his face was white as a ghost.

He blurted out, "What are you doing here?"

Since she often popped in unannounced to visit, Gina was puzzled by his strange question. "I was just in the neighborhood and wanted to stop by and tell you something."

Her dad looked at her with glazed eyes. "Yeah, well, you're never going to believe who just called me... Sandra."

Gina stared at him in disbelief.

"Dad! That's why I stopped by! I just saw her at her house for the first time in over 20 years!"

They stood there for a moment in complete silence, both contemplating the amazing coincidence, and then Gina asked, "What did she say?"

"She said she has found the Lord, and that she wants to meet me to return some things that belong to me. I agreed to see her tomorrow."

"No way, Dad. That is too bizarre", Gina replied. "Please do not give her my phone number. I do not want to talk to her."

The following morning, Gina's father met Sandra at her house, and he called Gina when he returned home. He told her that Sandra had found God after her own mother died. She sought help and her life had changed dramatically for the better in the last year. She had been diagnosed with bipolar disorder, and apologized profusely for her awful behavior.

"That would explain the wild mood swings and the Dr. Jekyll & Mr. Hyde behavior," Gina replied.

Tony went on to say that Sandra really wanted to talk with Gina.

"Dad, tell her I am really happy for her that she has found the Lord. Tell her I have forgiven her. I forgave her years ago, and I have no resentment or bitterness toward her," she said, "but please tell her that I have moved on with my life. I just don't want to talk to her and bring back painful memories."

"Do you want to know what she gave back to me?" he asked. "She gave me your mother's gold watch. She wants you to have it."

Gina could not hold back the tears. "I thought I would never see it again. I can't believe she didn't lose it or pawn it for drugs." After two decades, Gina finally had the one reminder of her mother she treasured most.

As the conversation closed, her dad said he was glad Gina had forgiven Sandra. But he said that maybe Sandra needed to hear that directly from Gina's own lips.

Gina said she would think it over, but in her heart she was certain she would never speak to Sandra. It was far too risky. But to keep up appearances, she told her dad to leave Sandra's phone number on the answering machine.

The following week, Mel Gibson's *The Passion of the Christ* came out. Because of our hectic schedules, Gina could not see it with the family, so she went to the movie alone when the kids were in school. As she sat in the darkened theater and watched the physical abuse Jesus endured, her own painful memories resurfaced. In the final scene when Jesus was hanging on the cross, Gina burst into tears as Christ looked at his tormentors with compassion and forgiveness.

"Maybe God is trying to get through to me about forgiveness," she thought. "Maybe Sandra *does* need to hear those words from me."

As she drove home that afternoon, her mind swirled with thoughts about Jesus, the movie, and Sandra. To escape them, she flipped on the radio. Don Henley's *The Heart of the Matter* was playing. It was as if God was speaking to her through the song: "But I think it's about forgiveness. Forgiveness. Even if, even if you don't love me anymore."

She looked up to heaven and said "Okay. I get it! I give up. I'll call Sandra when I get home!"

God was obviously speaking to my wife as he has so often spoken to me. And like me, Gina was, well, not exactly eager to obey.

Despite the many clear messages, Gina still did not want to talk to Sandra. She was being stubborn and figured she would do it later. Much later. Like when hell froze over.

As she walked into the house, she was happy to see that her new edition of *Today's Christian Woman* magazine had arrived. It would provide some much needed relief from the

Sandra problem. As she flipped through the stories, her eye caught something on page 52. The title of the article popped out at her: "Kate Didn't Even Like Her Stepmother – And Now God Wanted Her To Love Sandra?"

Gina could not believe it. She had never experienced God in this way. Too many "coincidences" were lining up too clearly. Even with her spiritual fingers in her spiritual ears, God's will was coming through loud and clear. She knew she had to call Sandra immediately. She dropped the magazine, picked up the phone and dialed the number her father had left.

Sandra answered the phone and Gina said, "Sandra, it's me, Gina."

Sandra paused on the other end of the line for a long moment, and said "Gina. I am so glad that you called. I have wanted to talk with you so badly."

They talked for quite a while. Sandra told Gina how she had found Jesus at the Mormon Church she attended. Although Gina understood the significant differences between mainstream Christianity and Mormonism, she was happy for Sandra that her life had turned around. Sandra also told her about the treatment she was receiving for her manic depressive illness. She told her how sorry she was for the terrible things she did to Gina when she was a young girl.

Sandra did not remember much about the actual abuse. She just kept apologizing, and Gina kept telling her that she had forgiven her long ago. Then the moment Gina dreaded most came. Nervously, Sandra asked if Gina would see her.

Gulping, Gina tried to think how to say "no" without hurting her feelings. Quickly, she blurted out that she would be down in Florida for a few weeks and maybe they could get together when she returned. Inwardly, she congratulated herself for wriggling out of the invitation. If they were to see each other it would have to be through divine intervention.

Gina thanked Sandra for keeping her mother's watch safe, told her she was glad they had spoken, and politely said goodbye. Gina felt a peace about the conversation, as if God had carefully inspired the words that would be said and the healing that would occur. Hanging up, she thought, "Wow. Forgiveness truly does release burdens."

Satisfied, Gina figured the story had played out to its dramatic conclusion. With the watch back in her possession and the dreaded phone call over, the case was closed. By the time she came back from Florida, Sandra would have forgotten all about getting together. Better yet, Sandra was moving out to Arizona in a few weeks and the meeting would be impossible.

But as John Lennon once said, "Life is what happens while you are busy making other plans."

Three days before leaving for Florida, Gina picked up our daughter Kira from a birthday party. Normally she would head back home the same way she came, but on this day, Kira wanted to pick up something from a store. So Gina hopped on the expressway and headed west. It was a beautiful, early spring day without a cloud in the sky. They were driving along in the right lane, talking about Kira's upcoming dance convention. Suddenly, an SUV traveling ahead of them in the fast lane veered sharply to the left and hit the median wall. Careening off the concrete barrier, it spun completely around several times right in front of them before crashing into the right wall of the below-ground highway. Gina immediately picked up the phone and dialed 9-1-1. She slowed down to a crawl but didn't want to stop completely because several other cars had already pulled over to help.

As she looked in the rear view mirror, she felt as if she were not in control of the steering wheel, and the car seemed to pull itself over to the right shoulder. Slamming the lever into park, she told Kira to stay in the car, and ran back to the crash site to check on the occupants. Gina saw the back end of the blue Jeep Cherokee was butted up against the wall and the front end stuck out in the right lane. As she approached the wreck, she looked at the woman in the passenger seat. Her body was contorted in pain, but even from 20 feet away, her face was unmistakable.

Staring in disbelief, Gina yelled out, "Sandra?!"

Groggily, Sandra looked out the window and focused on the woman coming toward her. Again she heard the voice, "Sandra? It's Gina!"

"Gina? Gina? Oh, my Lord! I must be dying. This is how your mother died. Am I dying?" she asked.

Gina could see Sandra was confused, disoriented, and probably in shock.

"No, you aren't dying Sandra. It's really me."

"What are you doing here?" Sandra asked.

"I was just driving and I saw your car hit the wall. I can't believe it's you."

Sandra could not believe it either. She started yelling to all of the bystanders that Gina was her daughter she had not seen in over 20 years. As this unlikely reunion was going on, Sandra's biological daughter, Courtney, was screaming hysterically. Gina ran around to the driver's side and grabbed Courtney's trembling hands. She didn't want to move her for fear she may have been seriously injured. Holding her hands, Gina prayed out loud to calm both of them down.

Back in our car, Kira was growing impatient. Wondering what was going on, she ran back to join her mother at the crash. Gina quickly introduced her, then told her to rush back to the car and call me at home. Kira dialed me immediately, and as she breathlessly reported the crash, I could not believe my ears.

When the ambulance arrived, Gina backed away as the paramedics worked on the injured victims. A few minutes later, a police officer approached the crowd calling out for Sandra's daughter. It didn't occur to Gina that they were talking about her, but when one of the men in the crowd pointed her out, the officer came up to her.

"Will you follow the ambulance to the hospital with your mom?" he asked.

Gina recoiled, "No, no, no! You don't understand. I haven't seen this woman in over 20 years. She is my stepmother. She needs her real family."

"Well, no one else is here right now. Will you just go to the hospital until someone else comes?"

Gina agreed and helped check Sandra and Courtney into the hospital. Gina and Kira sat and talked with Sandra for close to an hour. Sandra could not stop talking about how beautiful Kira was, and how sorry she was for the way she had treated Gina all those years. Gina told her over and over again that she had forgiven her long ago and honestly hoped Sandra had found happiness.

From her hospital bed, Sandra explained the harsh reality of being bipolar, and how the disease had caused other problems in her life. As Gina learned about the devastating effects of manic depression, she gained new perspective on the pain of her teenage years.

Despite the unusual circumstances, it was far more healing for Sandra to share with Gina face-to-face than over the phone. She even told Gina that she loved her. As my wife left the hospital that day, she basked in the warm glow that comes from being in the absolute center of God's will – even if only for a few unplanned moments.

To try to make sense of it all, Gina told our teaching pastor, Craig Mayes, the story. Like me, he was amazed at the entire sequence of circumstances, promptings, and strange occurrences. Gina asked him, "Did God cause the accident, or did he just know that it was going to happen and guide me to that exact time and place?"

Craig replied, "It has never been God's character to cause pain and suffering unjustly. But either way, it's clear that God's hand has been all over the entire sequence of events. The freeway miracle underscores just how important forgiveness is to God."

It's clear in the Bible that if we don't forgive, we become prisoners to negative thinking and bitterness. Unforgiveness hinders our spiritual growth and blunts our prayer life: *"And while you stand praying, if you hold anything against anyone, forgive him, so that your Father in heaven may forgive you your sins"* (Mark 11:25).

Many times we think we have *forgiven* when in fact we have probably just *forgotten*. True forgiveness includes a willingness to let the offending party know they have been freed. When it comes to forgiving someone, it's important that we not only "pray it", but "say it."

Even when it's creepy and awkward.

Forgiving a person who wrongs us sets us free. But it can also release the person who caused the pain. Whether we like to admit it or not, we all have caused pain in somebody else's life. And chances are, like Sandra, we've lived in slavery to those memories for too long. God has forgiven mankind through Jesus for the pain we have caused him over thousands of years. It was our mistakes and disobedience that put Jesus on the cross, but he forgave us anyway: *"Father, forgive them, for they do not know what they are doing"* (Luke 23:34).

If he can forgive us, surely we can forgive others. If God is bringing someone to your mind that you need to forgive, do it. If the thought of contacting them makes your skin crawl and your palms sweat, relax. That just means you're human.

Now get a grip. Gulp hard. Go do it: *"Forgive whatever grievances you may have against one another. Forgive as the Lord forgave you"* (Colossians 3:13).

And don't wait for New Year's Eve.

22

GRACE:
Wayward Son

Engines hummed. Passengers chatted. The beverage cart clattered by. But I was oblivious.

Staring out the window from my seat in aisle five, I barely noticed as the rugged terrain of the Continental Divide rolled under us, purple mountain's majesty and all. Returning from a business trip to northern Montana, I was trying to make sense of the turmoil brewing back home in Michigan. For the hundredth time, I mentally replayed the distressing phone call I received from my wife the night before.

She had gotten into an ugly argument with our 17-year-old son Chad. The trouble started when he forgot to pick up his younger sister from the dance studio. Bad move. Not as bad as robbing a liquor store, but bad enough. Gina was livid. She pulled out the angry-parent questions: "Who do you think you are? When are you going to grow up? When will you stop thinking about yourself and start thinking about others?"

Backed into a corner, Chad pulled out the angry-kid

defenses: "It's not my fault. You're always picking on me. You treat me like a child." He lashed out at his mother, his sister, and the stupid dance school. Nothing new about that. But when he insulted Kira for siding with their mom, it was the last straw for Gina. She got up within an inch of his face and demanded he leave the room until he could calm down.

It was the last straw for Chad as well.

With me safely across the country, he unloaded on Gina. He bellowed out how it was wrong for us not to trust him, how he was a pretty darn good kid, and how he deserved more freedom. Gaining momentum, he tested Gina with the old reliable "all my friends get to stay out as late as they want" line. When she didn't flinch, he blurted out that he could no longer handle living under our roof with our "restrictive rules."

Outburst over, he stomped up to his room, packed his duffle bag, and headed straight for the front door.

Reaching for the doorknob, he announced he was moving in with somebody else, somebody with more reasonable rules. Gina was heartbroken. But when he stepped through the door, she slammed it shut behind him, as if to say "I hope you find what you're looking for."

When my wife called me in Montana, she was worried sick. And rightly so. For the first time in our lives, we had no idea where our precious son was. We'd been praying for years that God would get hold of Chad's life, and quite frankly we were disappointed it hadn't happened according to our timetable.

Alone in my hotel room, I told Gina we just had to "trust that God would take care of him while he was gone." It wasn't very convincing – I barely believed it myself – but it sounded like something a strong father should say.

With our emotional gauges stuck somewhere between crying and cursing, we wearily acknowledged that all we could do for now was pray hard and hope for the best.

When we finished talking, it was one in the morning, Eastern Time. Gina was exhausted. I was drained. We agreed to postpone discussing our battle plan until I returned home. In an almost immediate answer to prayer, Chad called Gina the minute we hung up, and told her he was at his friend Chigo's house. He said he'd be staying there for "a while." Gina breathed a sigh of relief to know that at least temporarily, Chad was safe.

By the time morning dawned, Gina's relief had turned to anger. All she could think about was how ungrateful Chad was for the love we showed him and the upscale lifestyle we provided. He seemed oblivious to how fortunate we were as a family, and took for granted the many blessings God poured on our household.

Of all people Chad should have known better…

○   ○   ○

Just three months earlier, our family had taken a mission trip to Peru with 12 others from our church. Our job was to help Pastor Ramon install a wooden ceiling in his primitive church. It was an incredible adventure and an incredible eye-opener. My family saw firsthand how the average American lives like billionaire Donald Trump compared to people in the third world. Both of our kids experienced radical life change, but Chad was impacted the most. On our last night there, we attended a moving farewell ceremony. Halfway through, Gina tapped me on the shoulder and pointed toward our "too cool" teenager. Chad was flanked by several adoring Peruvian children, and tears were streaming down his face in a steady flow. I thought, *Surely God has gotten hold of him now.*

When we returned, we expected him to jump into God

with both feet. Instead, he jumped into the world, and it made for the worst summer in our family history. Chad repeatedly broke rules, rebelled against authority, and showed utter disregard for his parents. As a result, he had to deal with one bad consequence after another – some of them natural, some of them parentally imposed.

For me, his disrespect was by far the worst part. All I could think about was commandment number five from God's original Top Ten, *"Honor your father and your mother, so that you may live long in the land the Lord your God is giving you"* (Exodus 20:12).

Some 15 centuries later, Paul echoed and expanded on Moses' original text: *"Children, obey your parents in the Lord, for this is right. 'Honor your father and mother' – which is the first commandment with a promise –'that it may go well with you and that you may enjoy a long life on the earth'"* (Ephesians 6:1-3).

No wiggle room there. If honoring your parents was the single most important requirement for a long, bright future, Chad was in *big* trouble.

○   ○   ○

Looking at the towering cumulonimbus clouds outside the Boeing 757, my thoughts began wandering down the dark alleys of my mind. One worst-case scenario after another paraded across my imagination: Chad the drug dealer. Chad the cult leader. Chad the life insurance salesman (partially kidding).

Fear gripped me. I wondered where my son's disobedience would eventually lead him, and what it would take to turn his life around.

Because I am a male and therefore a "fixer," my anxiety soon turned to anger. If Chad was going to survive in this world, he would have to learn the Aretha Rule. You know, the one about R-E-S-P-E-C-T. But how to cultivate this parental respect? To quote Malcolm X, "By any means necessary." In my mind, this was my last, best chance to rescue my son before he went away to college.

Then it hit me.

Pulling my tray table down, I jotted down a brilliant idea – Gina and I would create a written contract for Chad. If he wanted back in *our* house, it would be on *our* terms, with his signature as evidence of his agreement with *our* rules. Like a wild horse that needed to be broken, Chad needed to be broken of his disrespect. Whatever it took, I would get a bit in this stallion's mouth and bridle him into submission for his own good.

Fortunately, God had a different plan that didn't involve boots and spurs. Unfortunately, I was almost too angry to hear it.

My agitation must have been visible because the usually friendly flight attendants were avoiding me. I was angry at my son for leaving, I was angry at myself for failing as a father, and I was angry at the stewardess for skipping my peanuts. Then at 30,000 feet above the Mississippi basin, God gave me a new kind of in-flight movie. All I could see in my mind was the image of a Jewish father, running down a dirt road to meet his prodigal son. Out of breath, the dad throws his arms around the boy and tells him how much he loves him.

Immediately, I recognized what God was up to. And – although I'm embarrassed to admit it – I had no inclination to obey. None. I responded with my usual pushback, *There is no way I am doing that God! You don't understand. This is different.*

I tried hitting the heavenly pause button, but God persisted. For the rest of the flight, all I could think about was the parable of the prodigal son that Jesus told his disciples.

In this well-known story, the arrogant son foolishly demands his family inheritance in advance and leaves home to be free of parental restraint. In a short time he squanders his fortune on wild living and is forced to work on a pig farm to survive. When he comes to his senses, he decides to face his father's wrath and return home – even if that means working for dad as a servant. The twist is that instead of punishing his wayward son, the father lavishly rewards him for returning.

The story really should have been called the prodigal *father*, because it's his generous, nonjudgmental response that holds the greatest truth: Love wins.

If there had been newspapers back in A.D. 33, the headline on the Monday after Resurrection Sunday should have proclaimed LOVE WINS in huge letters. And it should have been the same headline when the prodigal son's father did the unthinkable, *"Bring the best robe and put it on him. Put a ring on his finger and sandals on his feet. Bring the fatted calf and kill it. Let's have a feast and celebrate"* (Luke 15:22-24).

I may be slow on the draw but even I was beginning to see parallels: Jesus never gave us any conditions for our return to his household. He did not make us sign a contract before he took the nails in his hands on the cross. His voluntary death was an act of unselfish, unconditional forgiveness.

If Jesus could treat his enemies with that kind of love – after centuries of rebellion and sin – then surely I could do the same for my own son.

When I arrived home, Gina and I talked for hours. I told her how God had prompted me to apply grace instead of justice. At first, she had the same reaction I had – Chad's disobedience deserved a strong disciplinary response. But as she cooled down, I could tell that she was intrigued by the unusual response of the prodigal son's father. We agreed to pray about it over the next few days.

The following morning in my quiet time, I had trouble focusing on God. My mind kept wandering to my son's offense and the numerous options I had for killing him. I knew these negative thoughts weren't from God, but I could not get my mind off of punishing Chad. I hadn't spoken to him since leaving for Montana, and I had the overwhelming urge to call his cell and give him a piece of my mind.

I planned to spell out just how much he hurt his mother and me so he would never forget the repercussions of his actions. But somehow, despite my immaturity, God pressed through and calmed me down. Anxious thoughts disappeared. My pulse slowed. My head stopped pounding. And I sensed God whispering, *There is no need to call Chad. I'll take care of him while he's gone. Let me be his Father.*

Later that day, Gina called me at work. She was upset. She hadn't heard from Chad since his first call, and tomorrow was her birthday. She wondered what plans we should make. I told her that even if Chad did call, I didn't want him coming back on her birthday because it would be too disruptive. As we spoke, I wondered to myself if he would even remember her special day. *Probably not,* I thought, *he's too self-absorbed to think of anyone else right now.*

Hanging up the phone, I slipped right back into passing judgment on Chad. Can you say "relapse"? I wanted to call him in the worst way and yell, "Did you forget your mother's birthday tomorrow? I can't believe how selfish you are!" Again, God was there in the midst of my darkest thoughts, calming my spirit, *Don't worry. Chad is in my care. After all, I was his Father first.*

Each time I had the urge to call Chad, it got a little easier to put the phone down and trust God instead. I was slowly learning that he had Chad in his care. And I began to understand that maybe I had been subconsciously getting in

God's way regarding my son for years.

Here's what I mean: I knew I trusted God completely with my daughter and my wife. I trusted him totally with my job and my finances, too. But maybe, just maybe, I was holding back when it came to Chad. Unlike Abraham with his boy Isaac, I had never fully surrendered my firstborn son to God.

I wanted more than anything to see Chad commit his life to Christ, and I felt as his dad it was my responsibility to make it happen. In my zeal, I made all the classic "new Christian" mistakes: I threw scripture at him in the heat of debate. I warned him of doom and gloom if he disobeyed God. I labeled things he enjoyed as being from Satan. I had good intentions, but my parental scare tactics – and this is painful to admit – probably pushed him farther from God.

I know now that trying to attract someone to Jesus by fear and intimidation is like trying to make someone fall in love with you by using a Taser. It was the opposite of the "Love Wins" approach. And (surprise) it was failing perfectly.

Friday afternoon, Gina buzzed me to say that Chad had just called. To her amazement, he wished her a happy birthday and said he had a present for her. Since she wouldn't be home for several more hours he said he'd be happy to swing by and drop off the gift.

It was too good to be true. Then it got even better.

Chad told her he was ready to come home, but since it was her birthday, he didn't want to disrupt her day. He said he would come home around noon on Saturday. Then he added, "You won't believe what I've learned from God this week. I know I need to change, and I am ready to do just that."

I could hardly believe my ears. I was so thankful I had heard God and obeyed his leading to get out of the way and let him work on Chad's heart.

When Chad walked in the front door on Saturday, we wrapped our arms around him. We held that embrace for several minutes, telling him how much we loved him and how happy we were he was home. While we didn't kill a fatted calf (they're tough to find) we definitely celebrated his return.

With God's help, the usual parent-child communication barriers dissolved, defense shields came down, and we were able to simply talk about how to make things better. And talk we did.

The three of us went to the basement, sat on our coziest couch, and talked for three hours. Then Chad casually said the main reason he had come by the house on Wednesday was to get his Bible. *Whoa. Did I hear that right? Cue the hallelujahs!* He said he had sought God's advice throughout the week, and God had led him to several powerful teachings. One verse in particular stood out: *"Live as free men, but do not use your freedom as a cover-up for evil; live as servants of God. Show proper respect to everyone"* (1 Peter 2:16-17).

When I heard Chad quoting scripture, I was blown away that he sought answers from God and not his peers. He went on to explain how he observed the differences between us and his surrogate family during the week. The contrast helped him realize how much we truly loved him, and how blessed his family life was. He now understood we set rules because we loved him, not because we wanted to ruin his life.

The conversation was great. But something was obviously bothering Chad. Finally, he asked me why I didn't call during his absence. He was positive that I would. I confessed how badly I wanted to, but explained that God kept me from "getting in the way" of the lessons he wanted to impart directly to his prodigal son.

Chad agreed. He said that when I didn't call, it caused him to look inwardly to the things that were getting in the way of a better relationship between us. He realized that if his life was to be full of the blessings God promises, he needed to make some changes. Gina and I mostly just sat and listened, amazed how God had taken care of our son. And how much Chad had matured in such a short time.

With apologies to reading, writing, and arithmetic, Chad learned the other "three Rs." The ones we prodigals go through to enter God's kingdom: *running, reconciling,* and *restoration.* That week of the "three Rs" began a process of ongoing change for Chad as he continues to turn everything over to God. As a parent (and as a fellow prodigal) it's been encouraging to see how different his life has been since.

Truthfully, Chad wasn't the only one who had a meltdown followed by a breakthrough. I could have spared myself a lot of agony if I had just remembered the first big lesson I learned during Chad's "Journey to Manhood" ceremony. Four years earlier, when Chad and his sharp-shooting pals paintballed a guy's prize pickup truck, God prompted to me to *Say nothing.*

Which is, of course, just a nicer way of saying *Get out of the way.*

When I finally realized this was still his advice to me about Chad, I obeyed. My inner Bible thumper stopped thumping. All my years of worrying, nagging, and dragging him to youth groups were over. My efforts to push him to Christ fell by the wayside as I stepped back and allowed God to enter the picture. For a recovering control freak, surrendering *anything* is tough. When it's your one-and-only son you're giving up, it's impossible.

Unless you have help from the Father who did exactly that 2,000 years ago.

The Father of all fathers has been so faithful in my life, I've come to trust his voice. I know from personal experience that through him, all things are possible. Except when I take matters into my own hands.

When I do the listening and let him do the restoring, the results are amazing.

And love wins.

○　　○　　○

"Love is patient, love is kind. It does not envy, it does not boast, it is not proud. It is not rude, it is not self-seeking, it is not easily angered, it keeps no record of wrongs. Love does not delight in evil but rejoices with the truth. It always protects, always trusts, always hopes, always perseveres. Love never fails." (1 Corinthians 13:4-8)

23

RESTORATION:
Dead Man Walking

"Less than five minutes," the guide said. "That's how fast a school of piranha can strip the flesh off a 500-pound cow."

With razor-sharp teeth and an insatiable appetite, this tiny fish is nature's most efficient carnivore. A six-inch piranha can bite through a steel fishhook or a man's arm, and they'll attack anything that moves, regardless of size. A piranha's lower jaw juts out farther than its upper, making its triangular teeth fit together like a trap. Like a bulldog's, their oversize jaws are immensely powerful and conceal a set of sharp, pointed teeth. But unlike a canine, piranhas only use their teeth to cut and tear. Instead of chewing on the mailman's pant leg, they swallow their food whole.

Standing on the banks of the Nanay River in Peru, we listened as our native host warned how a single piranha bite can trigger a feeding frenzy. Baring his own uneven teeth, he described how quickly the calm water in front of us could be churned into a bloody foam. As he spoke, I took off my shoes and socks and waded out into the coffee-colored stream. Standing waist deep in the piranha infested water was clearly an act of insanity.

Or the prelude to a miracle…

○   ○   ○

Before embarking on my third mission trip to the Amazon jungle town of Iquitos, I had given each of my teammates an assignment: Bring a "life token" – a personal artifact that signified something in their life they wanted to give up to God and leave behind them forever in South America. This ceremony was a unique chance for Kensington students and leaders to figuratively (or literally) bury part of their past.

Our mission team started meeting early in January, six weeks before our departure. After the first meeting, our two college leaders, Tara and Anna, asked if a Peruvian friend of theirs could join us in Iquitos. His name was Manuel, and they had met him two years earlier when our church went to Lima. Manuel was an interpreter for the team, and the girls quickly became good friends with this likeable teen who was so enthusiastic about serving God. On our return trip to Iquitos the following year, we had to fly through Lima. During our layover, Tara and Anna squeezed in a visit with Manuel at the airport. Thrilled to reconnect with their bilingual buddy, they introduced me to him as we changed planes. Thinking I would never see the young man again, I quickly shook hands and moved on. But God (who is evidently way smarter than me) knew differently.

I told Tara and Anna that if Manuel could get himself up to Iquitos, I would be happy to have him join our team.

As usual on our journey to Iquitos, we had to fly through Lima, and we hooked up with Manuel there. We also had a chance to meet his mother and father. It was two in the morning, but the colorfully dressed couple made the long bus ride to see their son off. His parents seemed delighted and deeply grateful that we invited Manuel to join us on our trip.

Maybe too grateful.

While I didn't think much of it at the time, I noticed an odd look of yearning in their expression, a hint of unknowable sadness that seemed out of place at such a happy occasion.

The week in Iquitos was a happy blur. For the first two days, we worked in Pastor Ramon's church. Half the team worked on building a balcony and half worked on sanding, priming, and painting walls. Only three years earlier this church had been nothing but a tin shell and a hard-packed dirt floor. With financial help from the people of Kensington, Ramon's tireless volunteers had transformed it into a beautiful gathering place. It was humbling to see how our modest support had spurred such an amazing transformation.

We also had the chance to visit several remote churches planted by Pastor Ramon. Two were in tiny river villages and two were deep in the rain forest. On our rough and tumble journey out to the first village, I told the students how our task was directly linked to what the Apostle Paul experienced on his missionary journeys. We too were visiting fledgling congregations that were in need of our love, encouragement, and gifts.

The first church we visited was perched high on a hill overlooking the lush river valley below. It was called *Nuevo Retiro*, or New Retreat. The scenic views from inside the church were absolutely spectacular.

And absolutely unobstructed.

The members had run out of money after erecting just one wall. The four corner posts held up rough-hewn poles, partially covered with corrugated tin. That was it. One wall, half a roof, and no floor. But you could see in the hopeful faces of the villagers that someday it would be a finished house of worship. The pastor of *Nuevo Retiro* was the father of our friend Guido – the same young man my family was sending through school!

Guido's father Hector is a wonderful man, sincerely thankful for how God provides for him, his family, and his joyful open-air church. When our team gave him a stack of Peruvian *soles* worth about $500, he buried his head in my chest, hugged me tightly and wept. Hector's gratitude in the midst of grinding poverty was touching. Watching people gladly worship Jesus in a church with no water, no electricity, and no furniture reminded us how much we take for granted.

All week, our interpreter Manuel (aka "Manny") was a joy to be around. He had a cheerful personality, and a bright infectious smile. He loved to laugh. He played guitar and often led students in singing. He shared bits and pieces of his testimony with anyone who was interested. By all appearances he was rock solid in his faith. Despite the heat, humidity, and hard work, Manny seemed to truly be enjoying himself.

The entire week was full of "God moments" that built our faith, but it was the last 24 hours that put the exclamation point on the trip.

It started with Manny's life token story.

Manuel sat on the edge of the king-sized bed in our room at the Royal Inn Hotel in downtown Iquitos. Surrounding him, 17 students from our mission team completely occupied every inch of available space on the bed. If they were going to share deeply personal stories, they wanted to be physically close as well. As Rachel finished her story, it was time for Manny to share his life token with the team.

Because he had rendezvoused with our U.S. team when we landed in Iquitos, Manny had only a few days to think about what he wanted to "give up" and share with the group.

Up until this point in the evening, all the life token stories had been powerful and moving. But Manny's was more than inspiring. It was disturbing.

Without visible emotion, Manny handed over his cell phone to the students on the bed and said, "This is my life token. I want each of you to delete one of the pictures off of my phone, because they depict me living my old life. You see, for the last six months, I have wandered aimlessly back into my old world of street gangs and illegal drugs."

The hotel room reverberated with a collective gasp, then fell silent.

Manny began by sharing how he had become a successful youth pastor in Lima, and how energized he was to serve his church. In the Peruvian clergy, only the senior pastor draws a salary. So the youth pastor is an entirely volunteer position. Happy to work without pay, Manny considered it a great honor and a great learning experience for a young man working his way up in ministry. But when he stumbled and made one mistake, everything changed. Trust was broken. Friendships dissolved.

His career seemed over.

Incredibly, the church offered him no counseling, no support, and little hope for restoration. To Manny, it felt like the group that was so concerned about reaching others for Christ was turning their backs on him. The staff that was so eager to use his energy to build their youth ministry now seemed indifferent to his anguish. He couldn't have been more hurt by his co-workers if they had physically tortured him.

He was angry. He was humiliated. And worst of all, he began questioning his faith. Soon he was enticed by seeing the rich lifestyle and – even more tempting – the camaraderie his old friends enjoyed in the gang scene. Ironically, when the church failed him, the drug dealers embraced him. Before long he was plunged into a subculture of street crime, all-night partying, and self-destructive behavior.

The former youth worker went from a life of poverty and chastity to a life of easy income and easy women. Weapons, motorcycles, and flashy jewelry earned the gang members respect on the streets. But deep inside, Manny knew the truth about Jesus Christ and hated the double life he was leading. He told us how he had been tormented with evil thoughts, dark fears, and overpowering guilt.

Then he got an unexpected e-mail from Tara and Anna, inviting him to join us in Iquitos.

Looking directly at the two American girls, Manuel explained how much that invitation meant. It had literally given him life-sustaining hope for the past six weeks. All he could think about was our upcoming trip together to Iquitos. Now, having lived with us for a week, he said his head was spinning and his heart was broken. He observed how much we loved and cared for one another, encouraging each teammate in their individual faith journey. He said that it was our authenticity and genuine love that made him realize that maybe not all Christians were hypocrites. He was also amazed at how easily we all seemed to share our emotions and tears – especially the guys.

As we hung on his every word, Manny said his father was one of those *macho hombres* who teach their sons that real men don't cry. He said he had not shed a tear for over a decade. He was not even sure if he could anymore. In fact, he was telling us his own tragic story in a blasé, matter-of-fact manner.

And then he dropped the real bombshell. In a calm voice, Manny said he had developed a game plan right before he joined us in Iquitos. He figured that he would spend one last week with his old friends Tara and Anna, then go home and kill himself.

He stopped at that point in the story and paused. Everyone in the room froze. None of us could believe that the handsome young man sitting before us could have been secretly suffering so much emotional pain.

We sat motionless for what seemed like ten minutes of uncomfortable silence. Then we all had the same idea at once. We gathered around Manny, laid our hands on him and prayed. Each person in the room had something to say to God on behalf of Manny. And as we prayed for him, Manny began to cry for the first time in years.

As the love of Christ flowed through our hands and into him, years of repressed pain and sadness came pouring out. Soon the weeping turned into sobbing. He cried uncontrollably during the entire time we prayed for him. Locked in a group hug, we asked God to make this night a major turning point for Manny. Knowing he was experiencing the real love of Jesus Christ gave us hope that the old Manny was being buried in this hotel room and the new Manny would soon be rising from the spiritually dead.

Uttering our closing words, "In the precious name of your Son, Jesus Christ, we pray," we all sensed the intensity of a genuine God-drenched divine moment. We had come to Peru believing our only purpose was to help build churches, but God (who must chuckle sometimes) knew all along we would be his instruments to save a precious man's life.

The remaining life tokens took us well into the early morning hours, but none of us grew tired or restless as one story after another gave us a *grande* dose of hope and healing.

The next morning, we boarded long wooden canoes to visit a church in the village of Manicamiri on the Nanay River. Each 22-foot boat was powered by an ancient Evinrude outboard motor. When the guides pulled the rope starters, the two-stroke motors coughed blue smoke and sputtered into action. Fully loaded, the gunwales of the shallow draft canoes were only four inches above the surface. Dodging Annona roots and submerged stumps, the guides deftly threaded the needlelike crafts through unmarked channels used by the Indians for centuries.

Three hours later we put into a small clearing.

Earlier in the week, one of our students had asked if he could be baptized in the Nanay. What Keaton did not know was that his father, Owen, had planned a "Journey to Manhood" ceremony to celebrate his 16th birthday. After an emotional reading of letters detailing the character traits of a "real man," we walked Keaton down to the Nanay for his baptism. On the way down, I asked jokingly if there were any piranhas in the river. Guido looked at me and replied, "Oh yes, but just little ones."

That was not the answer I was looking for.

Owen and I quickly baptized Keaton. After invoking the name of the heavenly Father, the earthly father grabbed his son and scampered back to safety. But God didn't allow me to join them. Moments earlier, during Keaton's ceremony on shore, I had seen a supernatural vision of many others coming down into the river to be baptized.

As I stood alone in the brackish water, I felt prompted by God to ask if there were any others who felt a stirring to be baptized. But after waiting for an uncomfortable (and scary) minute or so, no one else spoke up. Miserable from the heat and half soaked with rainforest perspiration, I turned around and dove in to swim with the "little" piranhas. Completely submerged, I stroked and kicked and glided underwater until I thought my lungs would burst. It was incredibly refreshing, and when I reached shallow water I was relieved to see I still had all ten toes.

Heading for shore, I wondered, *Did I misunderstand God? Was my vision just wishful thinking?* As I climbed the muddy bank, one of our leaders, Rose, called out, "Wait, Jeff. There is one more."

I looked up to see a young girl walking to the water's edge, tears streaming down her face. When I recognized who it was, I also began to cry – Ashleigh was the first one I saw being baptized in my vision. She had come on the trip reluctantly, skeptical about who God was or if he even cared about her life. But somewhere south of the equator she experienced the kind of raw truth that's hard to explain until you experience it for yourself. And now here she was, getting baptized, publicly proclaiming her desire to follow Jesus for the rest of her life. It could not have been a more uplifting moment for me.

Except God wanted to make it even better.

Ashleigh triggered a steady stream of people coming into the water, starting with two young men from Pastor Ramon's church. Next came Pierre and Segundo, Peruvian believers we knew from previous visits. Others came, natives and Americans alike, finally ending with Annie, a devoted young follower who had never been baptized.

And then there was… Manny.

One week earlier he was running drugs with gangsters and pimps. Today he was stepping into the river to declare his recommitment to Jesus Christ. As he went under, the old Manny was washed away and the new Manny arose, clean and strong. It was an incredible ending to an incredible story.

We didn't plan it. We couldn't explain it. But we all knew that Manuel was freed from the prison of his past. And that he was going to shine like a beacon into the lives of those around him in Lima.

So why is it that mission trips seem so full of divine moments? Why do we experience more miracles in a week or two in the mission field than we do in a lifetime of daily humdrum?

I think it's because "out there" is where we come closest to living the life God designed us for: We spend our days dependent on Him – in scripture, prayer, and worship. We give of ourselves – our time, energy, and finances. And most importantly, we give our love. For a few short days or weeks, we live "other-centered," thinking very little about ourselves.

But there's another important ingredient – the love we receive. The people of Iquitos, both children and adults, are the most loving and joyful people I have known. With very little in the way of material possessions, they give freely of what they *do* have – a bumper crop of love, peace, and joy.

When we receive God's incredible gift of grace and love through Jesus, it overflows from our lives into others. In Peru, we were the recipients of God's abundant love all week, and it just naturally spilled over into anyone we came in contact with. Especially Manny.

And maybe even the piranhas.

○　○　○

"Dear friends, let us love one another, for love comes from God… Since God so loved us, we also ought to love one another. No one has ever seen God; but if we love one another, God lives in us and his love is made complete in us." (1 John 4:7, 11, 12)

24

LIFE:
Eyes On The Road, Ear To Heaven

In 1862, General Ulysses S. Grant led a decisive victory against the Confederate forces at Fort Donelson. The terms he sent to the defeated southern commander contained the first recorded use of the phrase "unconditional surrender." When journalists caught wind of his tough terms, they jokingly reported that Grant's first two initials stood for "Unconditional Surrender."

When the fort's commanding officer, General Buckner, signed Grant's papers of surrender, there were no compromises, no escape clause, and no loopholes. No deals were cut. No exclusions were made.

That's the way I want to surrender my life to God – completely and unconditionally.

I'm not there yet. There are days when I want my will to be done instead of his. There are days I don't seek him with all my heart. Days when I cram him in a box or ignore him. And plenty of days when I drown out his voice with a flurry of activity that somehow seems more important than listening.

But I'm making progress. With God's help, I've learned to dream bigger, love deeper, laugh harder, and pray longer. My devotion to my wife is stronger than ever. I'm not the perfect husband, but growing together in the reality of Jesus has strengthened our marriage. My relationship with my children is richer than ever. I'm not the perfect dad, but I've surrendered my personal ambitions so God can unfold his wonderful plan for their lives. I have formed lasting friendships with people from all walks of life. I have new brothers in India and Peru, in rural huts and suburban mansions. I have impacted the lives of former strangers. And they have impacted mine.

Most importantly, I have developed a close, intimate relationship with the living God who created the universe (how's *that* for name dropping?).

Before I got radically saved, I mocked people I thought went overboard with the whole "Jesus thing," echoing Karl Marx that "religion was opium for the masses." I half agreed with wrestler-turned-governor, Jesse Ventura, "Organized religion is a sham and a crutch for weak-minded people who need strength in numbers."

I thought people who claimed to have a "personal relationship" with God were lonely or loony.

Oddly, despite my cynicism, I conceded that Jesus might be the Son of God. And I had no problem with the virgin birth. I even believed he died on a cross. But I did not think I "needed him" in any way. Why should I?

Success came easy: I went to college, got a job, went to a prestigious business school, received my MBA, got a better job, bought a big house, got a promotion, bought a bigger house, wound up in the newspapers, and – realtors rejoice – bought an even bigger house. When it came to self-gratification, I put the boom in baby boomer.

It was the I-Me-Mine game plan and I was executing it

flawlessly. But as I said in the opening chapters, something was missing. I couldn't find the happiness that was supposed to come with success. Searching for peace of mind, we moved to the country so I could slow down and search for answers. But I was so full of myself that Jesus seemed irrelevant to my quest.

Little did I know, God had me right where he wanted me. When I finally discovered that Jesus was the "missing link," I accepted his invitation and surrendered my heart. Since then, my life – forgive the cliché – has never been the same.

As I've gotten to know Jesus better, I've learned that spiritual growth doesn't come by sheer willpower or good works. I can't just grit my teeth and resolve to "try harder" to be a better person. I can't do more "religious stuff" to impress the Lord. All I can do is draw closer to God, and when I do, he draws closer to me: *"Come near to God and he will come near to you"* (James 4:8).

I've also learned to be a fruit inspector.

I don't mean the kind that squeezes the melons at Kroger. I mean the kind that stands in front of his bathroom mirror and looks for evidence of Jesus staring back.

It's like this: The level of "fruit" in my attitude and actions is the best gauge for measuring my spiritual growth. If I am truly experiencing God, the evidence will be the fruit my life produces: *"But the fruit of the Spirit is love, joy, peace, patience, kindness, goodness, faithfulness, gentleness and self-control"* (Galatians 5:22-23).

When I'm Mr. Grinch to my kids or Johnny Rambo to an employee, I know I'm overdue to spend time with Jesus. When veins are popping out in my forehead because of a slow sales clerk, or my face is beet red and I'm pounding the dashboard because of a dimwitted driver, I know I need to chill out and seek God.

Recently, my son Chad asked me what year in the stock

market was the toughest of my career. I thought about it for a long moment, and replied "this year."

He looked at me in surprise and said, "Really? I would have never known. It sure hasn't seemed like it at home."

His response was evidence of the fruit in my life. Fruit like *peace* in the midst of economic chaos, *faith* in the midst of financial uncertainty, and *joy* in the midst of plunging portfolios. The simple fact that I didn't take the rotten economy out on my family was the result of planting seeds years earlier. I certainly don't produce that kind of fruit consistently, but at least I've seen a glimpse of how good life can be if I (the branch) abide in Jesus (the vine) daily (John 15:1-8).

On my spiritual journey, I've boiled most of what I've learned down to three critical truths.

First, I need to **shut up and listen**. The Holy Spirit is our guide and teacher, and he desires to be active in our lives. The night before his execution, Jesus promised his disciples that *"the Holy Spirit, whom the Father will send in my name, will teach you all things"* (John 14:26). He said the Spirit *"will guide you into all truth"* (John 16:13). Today, he guides us in the promptings, nudgings, and stirrings of the heart – signals I admit can be easy to miss if we are not proactively abiding in Jesus. Whether God is your pilot, your co-pilot, or just a passenger back in coach, is entirely up to you. He will not force you to listen to his flight plan. But rest assured fellow travelers, if you belong to the Shepherd, he *will* speak to you: *"My sheep listen to my voice; I know them and they follow me"* (John 10:27).

Second, God expects me to **respond and obey**. When God says "jump" I shouldn't say "how come?" but "how high?" Tempted by the same things that tempt us, Jesus set the perfect example of obedience, *"If you obey my commands, you will remain in my love, just as I have obeyed my Father's commands* *and remain in his love"* (John 15:10-12). And why wouldn't we obey? After all, whatever he asks us to do is out of love – for us and for others. Like a good soldier, I obey God even if I don't completely understand (or agree with) his orders because I know my commanding officer loves me.

Despite the fact that he is all-powerful, God is not like some Marine drill sergeant who yells louder and louder to intimidate a recruit into blind obedience. On the contrary, if we repeatedly fail to respond, his voice will become fainter and harder to hear. If we ignore him long enough, we build up a "spiritual callous" that can make us almost immune to his promptings. On the other hand, if we do respond, he'll continue to use us in even more powerful ways: *"Well done, good and faithful servant! You have been faithful with a few things; I will put you in charge of many things"* (Matthew 25:21).

Third – and this is most important – I need to **fully surrender**. I love the old Methodist hymn written by Judson Van Deventer called *I Surrender All*. But to be totally honest, I should sing it "I surrender some." Too often I allow myself to be distracted or tempted away from full surrender. Because of selfishness, fear, or stubbornness, I sometimes hold back part of my heart.

But Jesus left no room for part-time devotion: *"'Love the Lord your God with all your heart and with all your soul and with all your mind... and love your neighbor as yourself'"* (Matthew 22:37-39). According to him, surrendering our lives means to love God with every fiber of our being and to love others as much as we love ourselves.

But how? Actually, it's pretty simple. Not easy, but simple. All living things grow. Kids, pets, mold in the fridge, whatever. So we should expect growth in our relationship with Jesus, too. Surrendering to God's will and becoming more "Christ-like" are the results of loving God *"with all your heart."*

Reality check: This kind of love doesn't come naturally or through human effort. We have to ask the Holy Spirit living in our hearts to help us love God. Only he can give us the desire and the ability to love God and others. In its natural unregenerate state, the human heart is *"deceitful above all things"* (Jeremiah 17:9), and not affectionate toward God, *"the sinful mind is hostile to God"* (Romans 8:7). We don't love God on our own, and quite honestly, we don't even *want* to. And we sure as heck don't love our neighbors. Only God's grace can change our hearts so he can use us to change the world.

Which is the whole point of **listening, responding,** and **surrendering.**

Because like it or not, you and I are God's only plan for sharing his love with a world that desperately needs his forgiveness and hope. There is no Plan B. If Jesus believes in you and me that much, maybe we ought to believe in him enough to stick our necks out and love him unabashedly, unashamedly, insanely, and without reserve. Even nonbelievers are attracted to the absolute beauty and undeniable power of this kind of crazy, irrational, overwhelming love.

Back in 1967, the Beatles debuted the song *All You Need Is Love* on the first global television link in history. Beamed by satellite to 26 countries, John Lennon's composition was heard by 350 million people simultaneously. Although not a religious man, the songwriter stumbled onto something universal and powerful that resonates throughout scripture: *"God is love"* (1 John 4:16), *"Love never fails"* (1 Corinthians 13:8), and *"Love covers over a multitude of sins"* (1 Peter 4:8).

Penned at the height of the hippie "peace and love" movement, Lennon's hopeful lyrics seem naïve in today's cynical world, but they're just as true today as they were then. All we need *is* love. God's love.

A loving heart that is "unconditionally surrendered" is

the heart God can use for his purpose. When we seek him daily by praying, worshipping, and reading the Bible, he will begin to stir in our hearts. When we quietly listen for his voice with all our heart, he promises to show up: *"Then you will call upon me and come and pray to me, and I will listen to you. You will seek me and find me when you seek me with all your heart"* (Jeremiah 29:12-14).

Caution! Listening, responding, and surrendering may be hazardous to your comfortable lifestyle and status quo...

○   ○   ○

Digging my toes into the warm sand, I was lounging like a pro in my beach chair on Sanibel Island. It was Easter break 2004, and the sun was perfect. The waves rolling in from the Gulf of Mexico blotted out the voices of my wife and her friends as they chatted about whatever women chat about. I was well into a book and not paying attention to anything except the tiny umbrella in my drink. Frankly, I'm one of those guys that can't sit still on the beach longer than 22 minutes. I'd rather walk, swim, shell, or build sandcastles than just sit in the sun and talk about... nothing.

But on this particular afternoon, the talk was about *something*. Gina was telling her friends that Kensington was thinking about planting their next campus in the western suburbs. I half-dozed as she rattled off a dozen areas being considered. Suddenly, the noise of wind and surf abated and I clearly heard Gina mention the town we had left several years before. When I heard the name of our hometown, my heart jumped out of my chest like Pepe Le Pew sighting the black and white female cat.

Like the hot-blooded skunk, I sat bolt upright and shouted, "Really?"

From that exact moment on the Florida beach, I knew God had laid the people of our old stomping grounds on my heart. And that profound sense of mission has never left, no matter how hard I've tried to push it away. During the following months in my prayer time, God reminded me over and over again of who I was before I met him – and where my change had taken place. The equation was so basic I couldn't ignore it: If God could use Kensington to reach me, he could use it to reach the others *like* me I had left behind.

But as usual, I started whining: "Why me? Why now? We don't even live there anymore. We love our current church. And by the way, God, I definitely don't want to move back."

Thankfully, God has always been gentle with me when I'm cranky. In my quiet time with him he showed me a parade of faces, reminding me of old friends in the area who didn't know God's love. And to be honest, he never said anything about moving, just ministering. With the simple words *"Follow me,"* God was leading us back to our birthplace to reach others for him. From the city to the country to the city – only he could come up with a boomerang plan like that. And I had no choice but to obey.

Later that summer, we were invited to dinner with some friends in our old neighborhood. At the gathering, we met the McCormicks, a couple who were relatively new to the area. As we talked, we discovered they were also believers, and trying hard not to be sucked into the Paris Hilton lifestyle of this affluent ZIP code. Laughing, they told us that when they were introduced at cocktail parties, people inevitably asked which country club they belonged to. Their response was refreshing: "We can barely pay our property taxes here, let alone country club dues!"

That honest answer showed us they were authentic people who didn't take themselves or their prosperity too seriously. We identified with them instantly, and knew we'd become friends. We also found out that they had a real heart for the lost people in their community, and, in fact, dreamed about forming a new kind of church that would appeal to their un-churched neighbors.

On the way home that evening, I felt stronger than ever that God was leading me to help start a Kensington-style church in my old neighborhood.

Unfortunately, in the words of the Righteous Brothers' *Unchained Melody*, I was in for a "long, lonely time."

For several frustrating months, I felt like I was spinning my wheels. Nobody I spoke to would make a firm commitment. Even my wife was skeptical. I felt like a congregation of one. Finally, just after Easter break 2005, I received a phone call that confirmed my prompting from God. The McCormicks phoned to ask if they could help launch "Kensington West." For weeks, I had been praying for this specific family to have clarity on how and where they were to use their obvious gifts for God. When the call came, I put the phone aside, looked up to the sky and sighed "You are an amazing God."

From that point on, our core team began to take shape as dozens of other couples with strong leadership gifts stepped up to say they too felt called to help start this brand new church. That same summer we had a party to gauge interest in this fledgling vision. Over 125 people came, all feeling the same stirring in their hearts. Today, we are over 300 strong and less than a year away from our launch. Nobody in our K-West gang knows exactly where God is leading us, but we do know this: Starting a new church is scary, expensive, and exhausting. It's time consuming, stressful, and there's no guarantee it's going to be successful. But we also know we've heard from heaven.

○　　○　　○

God speaks in so many ways. On that picture-perfect day on the beach, he spoke through my wife. In that instant, he impressed something new and unexpected onto my heart and he's never let it slip away. When I hear God's voice, I know I can trust him, no matter where the adventure will lead, how much work it will take, or what disruption to my plans is involved. My heart has been conditioned to listen, respond, and surrender – to follow God into the unknown, knowing only that whatever he has planned for me is infinitely better than anything I could come up with.

If using expressions like "hearing God's voice" makes you nervous, I understand. And if you're skeptical about my "conversations with God," I don't blame you. After all, I freely admit I'm not a pastor, priest, or rabbi (I've never even played one on TV). But plenty of actual theologians – guys who know Greek and Hebrew and Billy Graham's cell phone number – have debated this issue till they're blue in the face and still can't agree. So while they're off theorizing on a cloud somewhere, I'm down here on street level just trying to intersect with the hurting people God tells me to help.

Anyway, I've already asked myself every question you could come up with at least a thousand times: *Why would God choose me? Could the voice in my head be just my imagination? Do my own subconscious desires affect my interpretation of the promptings? Is this whole thing for real?*

My answer to you is a lot like Jaya's answer to me when I asked him what life was like in India. He simply replied *"Come and see for yourself."*

Seeing for yourself requires a mix of common sense and common courtesy. Before you can expect a meaningful conversation with anyone (including God) you need to take the time to get to know them. Learn who they are and how they do things. Learn about their character, their personality, and what they expect from you. In God's case, this takes Bible study and prayer. When you're developing a relationship with anyone (especially God) there's no magic button to speed up the process.

Over the years, people have asked me, "How can I tell if God is speaking to *me?*"

I answer that question with another question, "If God did try to speak to you, could he get a word in edgewise?"

Before we can hear the other half of any conversation, we've got to stop blabbing and listen. Which is harder than you might imagine. We've been conditioned to think silence is bad so we block it out with noise. Any noise. TV, radio, boom box, iPod, Bluetooth, whatever. And if – God forbid – there's a brief lull in the conversation, we get squirmy. We'll blurt out just about anything to fill the dead air.

In my private prayer time, I spend half the session in silence, quietly meditating on scripture, with no agenda except to enjoy God's presence, *"My soul waits for the Lord more than watchmen wait for the morning"* (Psalm 130:6). Whether he chooses to break the silence or not is his business. But I provide him the opportunity at least once a day: *"Be still and know that I am God"* (Psalm 46:10).

o   o   o

Okay, I see your hand up in the back there: "What if I don't hear God? Am I an inferior Christian?"

Not at all. He loves us equally. *"God does not show favoritism"* (Acts 10:34). But don't be too quick to assume nothing's happening. Give God time and don't give up.

You there in the sweater: "What if some evil spirit or dark angel masquerades as God to trick me?"

Here's the test – God will never tell you anything that

contradicts the Bible. If something is immoral or unethical or doesn't line up 100 percent with scripture, reject it outright. Ask God to give you discernment.

Alright, the guy in the front row: "If I do what you do, am I guaranteed to hear from God?"

Nope, he's sovereign. But if you concentrate on improving the relationship instead of hearing from God, I *can* guarantee you'll grow spiritually and have a richer, more fulfilling life. The alliterative principles of listening, learning, and loving will bless you no matter what else happens.

○   ○   ○

Don't be discouraged if your experience is different than mine. God is all about communicating with his creation in lots of different ways: He spoke to Daniel in dreams. He got Moses' attention with a burning bush. He crashed King Belshazzar's party with a ghostly finger writing on the wall. He even spoke to Balaam through a donkey.

And if he chooses, he can reach us the old fashioned way – through our eardrums. One night, the young prophet-to-be Samuel was awakened by a voice he assumed was his boss, the high priest. When he ran to Eli, the elderly priest told him to go back to bed. When Samuel heard the voice again, he returned to Eli who just scowled and rolled over. By the third time his 12-year-old assistant woke him up, the old priest figured out who was interrupting the boy's sleep: *"Then Eli realized that the Lord was calling the boy."* With advice that's still good today, Eli told Samuel what to say if he heard the mystery voice again: *"Speak, Lord, for your servant is listening"* (1 Samuel 3:8,9).

He did listen, and because he was so wide open to hearing from God, Samuel spent the rest of his life communicating the Lord's vital messages to Israel.

So don't be surprised if he chooses to talk to you through the Bible, or other people, or circumstances, or even an audible voice. And don't be surprised if you take a little heat for saying you hear from God. Before it started happening to me over and over, I would have agreed with comedian Lily Tomlin: "When we talk to God, we're praying. When God talks to us, we're schizophrenic."

But what's a little razzing compared to the honor of serving a king? If you're ready to please God rather than men, if you're ready to trade your comfort zone for the danger zone, you're probably closer than you think to a conversational relationship with the Almighty.

Wherever you are on your spiritual journey, you can make yourself available for God's purpose by praying something like this from your heart:

*"Father, I pray that I will seek you with all my heart. I pray that I will **hear** your voice, **respond** to your promptings, and **surrender** to your will. Use me to accomplish your plan on the earth with the gifts and talents you've given me. Help me to quit trying to be my own boss and give my life over to your control. Speak as loudly as needed to get my attention, and use any means necessary to draw me closer to you. I ask this in the precious name of your Son, Jesus Christ. Amen."*

Now, shut the door, get quiet, and listen up. The next sound you hear just might be God.

MOSES, ELIJAH... AND JEFF
Epilogue by Craig Mayes

Does God still speak? If so, who does he talk to? And when someone claims they've heard from God, how can we know if it's true?

As a young follower of Jesus, I was taught – and believed – that God has already said all he has to say to us. I learned the Bible is the accurate and reliable record of God's final communication to humans. He had spoken directly to the prophets and apostles thousands of years ago, and speaks to us today only through their written words.

God's "silence" explained my denomination's strong emphasis on the Bible as the center of our faith. We read it, studied it, memorized it, and taught it. As "people of the Word," we prided ourselves on knowing that what we believed was accurate and right and complete.

Without realizing it, we were dangerously close to worshipping the Bible more than the one who wrote it. This attitude is nothing new. Jesus challenged the Bible deists of his day: *"You have never heard his voice nor seen his form, nor does his word dwell in you, for you do not believe the one he sent. You diligently study the Scriptures because you think that by them you possess eternal life. These are the Scriptures that testify about me, yet you refuse to come to me to have life"* (John 5:37-40).

Since then, my own experience has taught me that God – by his very nature – is a being who speaks. Jesus is called the full expression of God and is also revealed as the Word of God: *"In the beginning was the Word, and the Word was with God, and the Word was God"* (John 1:1).

We urge people to have a "personal relationship" with Jesus, but how can any relationship be personal without consistent and clear communication? In *Love Beyond Reason*,

John Ortberg says, "If I am to have a relationship with God that is in any sense personal, I must be open to the possibility that sometimes God does speak directly to me."

No doubt that sounds too mystical for many church leaders. If so, it's because naturalism has invaded the arena of faith. Imagine Christians who worship an immortal, invisible, miracle-working God being so squeamish about the supernatural!

To paraphrase comedian Jeff Foxworthy, "You might be a naturalist if... you think God is limited to the laws of nature or the precepts of science."

Consider a few widely accepted truths of Christianity:

1) God is all powerful and all knowing
2) God is everywhere at once
3) God hears everyone's prayers simultaneously
4) God indwells believers
5) God sends invisible angels to assist us

That all sounds pretty *mystical* to me. But the Bible we hold in such high regard tells us these strange-sounding things are absolutely true. So why be surprised to hear that God speaks directly to someone today?

I believe Jesus has invited us into a personal, interactive relationship, with him speaking and us listening: *"My sheep listen to my voice; I know them, and they follow me"* (John 10:27).

My travels to India helped me understand the concept of Jesus as the good shepherd. In the dusty streets of Andhra Pradesh (where there are as many animals as cars) I noticed a peculiar difference between goat-herders and sheep-herders.

Goat-herders walk *behind* their flock, yelling and using their staff to strike any goat that wanders off. These "bad shepherds" use fear and intimidation to keep their flock moving.

By contrast, sheep-herders lead by walking in *front*, gently guiding their flock by example. These "good shepherds" never shout. Instead, they speak softly to their flock, who – despite the noisy motor scooters and blaring car horns – can always recognize the still small voice of their shepherd.

But it doesn't stop with hearing. Jesus said his sheep not only listen to his voice, they follow him. Together, these two things define what it means to be a modern disciple – learning to distinguish the voice of Jesus, then doing what he says.

Wavelength is nothing more than one man's desire to live this out: to cultivate the ability to "tune in" God's voice (on a regular basis), then courageously follow wherever he leads. As Jeff's longtime friend, I've noticed there is one thing that makes his relationship with God so unique – he *expects* the Holy Spirit to speak to him.

Because of that conviction, he schedules specific quiet times each day to slow down and listen. Jesus said *"he calls his own sheep by name and leads them out"* (John 10:3).

So the question is not so much "Is God speaking?" but "Are we listening?" Jeff has shown what happens when an ordinary average man – not a prophet or apostle – listens and responds.

Hopefully, Jeff's adventures have made you at least wonder if God is speaking to you as well. I challenge you to spend time listening for the voice of the shepherd. And I pray that you and I will have the courage to respond when God asks us to be his arms and legs and hands on the earth.

Without this two-way communication, we may find ourselves living in *religion* and missing the *relationship*.

About The Authors

Jeff Petherick is a portfolio manager and partner in a top-ranked investment firm. When he's not busy picking stocks, he teaches seminars about Jesus and travels the world on mission trips. An avid outdoorsman, Jeff lives in a rural area north of Detroit with his wife and two kids. This is his first book that didn't involve paste and crayons, and was written to prove that ordinary men can do extraordinary things – when they obey the voice of God.

Karl Nilsson is the communication director for one of America's largest churches. Before working in the ecclesiastical realm, he operated a successful advertising agency. Prior to his career in marketing, he was a syndicated cartoonist, newspaper columnist, and magazine editor. Rejecting the starving artist cliché, he currently lives in a way-too-fancy-for-his-income suburb of Detroit with his wife and two children.